The Expert's Guide to

HANDGUN MARKSMANSHIP

For Self-Defense, Target Shooting, and Hunting

SELECTIONS FROM THE WRITINGS OF

Charles Askins, Jr.
Jeff Cooper
Julian S. Hatcher
A. L. A. Himmelwright
Jack O'Connor
William Reichenbach

and from
U.S. Army Field Manuals

JIM CASADA

Skyhorse Publishing

CONTENTS

◈◈◈◈

Askins on Pistols & Revolvers • HUNTING SIGHTS,
Charles Askins, Jr., *Colonel Askins on Pistols
& Revolvers*

HUNTING WITH THE HANDGUN, Jeff Cooper, in Jack
O'Connor, *Complete Book of Shooting* • HUNTING
WITH THE HANDGUN, Charles Askins, Jr., *The
Pistol Shooter's Book*

INTRODUCTION

THE PURPOSE OF THIS BOOK

This book is about target shooting with a handgun (with the exception of a small section on handgun hunting, which for most of us is only an infrequent activity). However, in my opinion, the popularity of target shooting with a handgun belies, or is incidental to, the overriding reason people are buying, owning, and training themselves in the use of handguns in ever-growing numbers — self-defense.

During the last century or so, by far the most popular use of the handgun has been for target shooting. It is estimated that several million Americans engage in the sport of shooting at targets simply for practice, for pleasure, or to engage in competition matches. Likely every small town in America has at least one handgun shooting range.

But today, as law-abiding Americans witness the rise of violent crime in their neighborhoods, the increased use of guns by criminals, the higher rates of recidivism among our prison populations, and the pardons of many violent felons, many of our citizens are turning to another important use of the handgun: self-defense. And it is to that purpose that this book is dedicated: to school you in handgun target shooting in order to equip you with the skills to effectively defend yourself and others against felonious attack.

The handgun is the ideal tool for self-defense. It is relatively short and small, can be operated with one hand if necessary, can be conveniently stored and carried, and, unlike a rifle or shotgun, can be brought into action and used in the close confines of a room in your home, or even your automobile.

But if a handgun has to be used, it has to be used effectively; that is, *accurately*. The irresponsible discharge of a handgun in untrained hands is like the detonation of a stick of dynamite. Its effects are random, unpredictable, and potentially deadly.

This is an awesome personal responsibility. You would not be taking the time to read this book if you did not agree. And to meet that responsibility, *you must train yourself in the effective and accurate use of the handgun.* This requires two things. First, you must study and learn the principles of handgun marksmanship set forth in the following pages. Second, you must put these principles into action with repetitive sessions of handgun target shooting on the range. Mastering handgun marksmanship by target shooting — at whatever distance and degree of accuracy you wish to achieve — is the absolute prerequisite to the effective use of the handgun in defense of yourself and others.

A Brief History of the Handgun

For centuries wars were won and men died by the sword. All of that changed with the invention of gunpowder sometime during the twelfth or thirteenth century, followed by the invention of cannons, muskets, and handguns sometime during the fourteenth century.

Since then, the handgun has acquired more notoriety than any other type of firearm, probably because of its association with a number of famous historical events, including the duel in 1804 between Alexander Hamilton and Aaron Burr that resulted in Hamilton's death; the death of Russian poet Alexander Pushkin in an 1837 duel; the battles of the American Civil War, during which prolific use of the handgun by Union and Confederate forces became widespread; John Wilkes Booth's assassination of Abraham Lincoln in 1865 (with a Philadelphia derringer); and the legendary encounters between gunslingers and lawmen on our western frontier in the 1900s.

At first, handguns were crude, almost toylike, unreliable weapons. But over time a series of changes were made that improved reliability. Chief among these were firing mechanisms that ignited gunpowder to create the energy to propel a lead ball down the barrel — first the *matchlock,* which used match cord to ignite gunpowder in a flash pan; then the *wheel lock,* which created sparks to ignite the powder; followed by *snap lock, snaphaunce,* and *flintlock* designs, which utilized a variety of hammer devices to strike a small piece of flint to produce ignition. These handgun ignition mechanisms prevailed for nearly two hundred years, even though they were frequently subject to misfire and had the disadvantage in night combat of revealing the shooter's position by the flash of the igniting gunpowder.

These deficiencies were cured in 1807 when the Scottish minister Alexander John Forsyth invented the percussion-cap lock, in which the firing mechanism no longer used a flash pan, but rather a tube leading straight into the gun barrel to ignite a cap that exploded when struck. Caplock revolvers proved to be a tactical success in the Civil War, when thousands were used by both Union and Confederate forces.

Thereafter, throughout the balance of the nineteenth century and into the twentieth century, in America as well as Europe, numerous new handgun mechanisms were invented, including single- and double-action revolvers, the Lee box magazine, semiautomatic mechanisms, and both rimfire and centerfire handgun cartridges.

In America, four handgun designs are worthy of special mention.

First, and unquestionably the most famous handgun design in American history, is that of Samuel Colt, including the 1836 Colt Paterson revolver and its famous successors: Colt's Walker Army revolvers, used by the U.S. Cavalry in the Mexican War of 1846–1848; and Colt's Navy or 1851 Colt model.

Another enduring American handgun design was that of John Browning, the 1911 Colt .45, made famous by its tremendous stopping power when used by the U.S. Army against Moro guerrillas in the Philippines at the turn of the twentieth century.

In 1915, John Browning also invented the Colt Woodsman .22 semiautomatic rimfire pistol, which for years was the favorite handgun of target shooters.

A fourth lasting American handgun design is Elmer Keith's and Philip B. Sharpe's 1934 Smith & Wesson .357 Magnum of *Dirty Harry* fame.

Arms manufacturers in Europe also created several legendary handguns. Likely the most famous European handgun is the German Luger, first introduced in 1902. The Luger, also known as the 9 mm Parabellum (the name Parabellum comes from the Latin phrase *Si vis pacem, para bellum* — "If you wish peace, prepare for war"), was followed in 1906 by the world-famous Luger model, Pistole .08.

Use by a young Winston Churchill in the Battle of Omdurman in Sudan in 1898 brought fame to the Mauser C96 "Broomhandle," the first reliable semiautomatic pistol. (The pistol's unusual name derives from the handgun's cumbersome grip.)

In 1929, the German firm of Carl Walther Waffenfabrik invented what experts at the time considered an even more reliable semiautomatic, the Walther Model PP (Polizei Pistole).

In 1982, Austrian Gaston Glock introduced his revolutionary polymer design, the Glock 17. Since then, the Glock firm has manufactured an astounding 2,500,000 pistols in a variety of models and calibers. The Glock is the handgun of choice for scores of armies and police forces around the world. Today it commands sixty-five percent of the handgun market share in the United States.

For target shooting up to hunting big game as large as bears — from the lightest single-shot rimfire .22 target pistol up to the awesome Smith & Wesson .500 Magnum revolver (which when loaded with five two-inch .50 caliber cartridges weighs five pounds!) — there are available today a wide variety of handgun designs in a wide variety of calibers and ammunition loads, from numerous American and international arms manufacturers, among them Armalite; Armscor; Astra; Beretta; Bersa; Browning; Ceská Zbrojovka; Charter Arms; Cimarron; Colt; Dan Wesson; FNH; Freedom Arms; Glock; Heckler & Koch; High-Point; Hi-Standard; Iver Johnson; Kahr Arms; Kimber; Makarov; North American Arms; Para; Remington; Rohrbaugh; Rossi; Savage; SIG Sauer; Springfield Armory; Steyr; Sturm, Ruger & Co.; Taurus; Thompson/Center; Uberti; U.S. Firearms; Walther; and Webley & Scott.

All of these manufacturers now maintain web sites where you can acquaint yourself with the specifications and prices of their handgun models.

I
HANDGUN BASICS

With handguns, to an even greater extent than with long guns, mastery of marksmanship begins with the basics. Arguments on the best grip and stance will endure as long as the sport itself, but no matter what the individual handgunner's preferences when it comes to these and related matters, getting them right and performing them in a consistent fashion is of paramount importance. Those of us who have watched too many shoot-'em-up westerns may be inclined to think that accuracy with a handgun goes right along with lightning-fast draws and revolvers fanned so rapidly they might be mistaken for semiautomatics.

In truth, sure and steady wins the marksman's prize in most cases, and anyone who has doubts in that regard needs to visit the site of the famed shootout at the OK Corral. How anyone came out of the tight quarters — almost point-blank range — of that gun battle is amazing. Or, to put matters in another perspective, the gunslingers who were present proved beyond doubt that they were anything but superb marksmen.

Here the incomparable Jack O'Connor (first and foremost a rifleman, but an individual who knew a great deal about all types of firearms)

*and four noted authorities on handgun marks-
manship look at some of the key factors in accurate shooting with pistols and revolvers.*

●

In this piece from his Textbook of Pistols and
Revolvers *(1935), Julian S. Hatcher takes a careful, considered look at the pros and cons of the
two basic types of handguns. It should be noted
that his use of the word* automatic *to describe*
pistols that used clips or magazines was com-
monplace in the era during which he wrote. In
today's parlance, the proper description would be
"semiautomatic" (meaning a new squeeze of the
trigger is required to fire each round). Hatcher's
evaluation of types of handguns is a sensible one,
and shooters contemplating purchase of such a
firearm would be well advised, before spending
their hard-earned cash, to consider what he has
to say about the merits of each type.*

**Expert
Julian S.
Hatcher
examines
the pros
and cons of
pistols and
revolvers**

REVOLVER VS. AUTOMATIC PISTOL

In late years there has been a great deal of dis-
cussion as to the relative merits of the revolver
and the automatic pistol. A great host of automatic pistols have been invented and manufactured with varying degrees of success. In military
sizes the automatics have reached the greatest
perfection, and have been adopted by the United
States Army, and by many other important

armies. In pocket sizes automatic pistols are sold throughout the world in very large numbers. Nevertheless, the revolver has been holding its own during all this period, and is now manufactured in quantities apparently as large as ever. It is difficult to say which is actually better, the revolver or the automatic pistol. Each has its own distinct advantages and. disadvantages, which the reader must decide for himself. I will enumerate some of the advantages and disadvantages of each type of weapon.

The revolver has the following advantages: **Advantages of the revolver**

1. It is an old standard weapon, everyone is used to it, and most everyone knows something about how to handle it.
2. The revolver is safer for inexperienced people to handle and to carry than the automatic pistol.
3. The mechanism of a revolver allows the trigger pull to be better than that of the average automatic.
4. A misfire does not put a revolver out of action.
5. A revolver will handle satisfactorily old or partly deteriorated ammunition which gives reduced velocities that would jam an automatic.

Among the principal disadvantages of a revolver as compared to an automatic are the following:

Disadvantages of the revolver

1. It is more bulky to carry.
2. The grip is generally not as good.
3. It is slower to load.
4. It is hard to clean after firing.
5. It is harder to replace worn or broken parts on a revolver than on an automatic.
6. Replacement of a worn or corroded barrel is a factory job.
7. Worn or poorly made weapons are subject to variable accuracy, due to improperly lining up cylinder or due to not locking cylinder properly in line with barrel.

Advantages of the pistol

The advantages of the automatic pistol are:

1. It has a better grip — fits the hand and points naturally.
2. It is more compact for the same power.
3. It is easier to load than a revolver.
4. It is easier to clean.
5. In case of a worn or corroded barrel a new one can be put in at small expense without sending the gun to the factory.
6. It gives a greater number of shots for one loading than a revolver.
7. It gives greater rapidity of fire and greater ease of rapid fire.
8. There is no gas leakage or shaving of bullets.

The automatic pistol, on the other hand, has some serious disadvantages, among which are the following:

1. The ammunition must be perfect. Old and deteriorated ammunition will cause a jam.
2. A misfire stops the functioning of the gun.
3. When the gun is kept loaded for long periods of time the magazine spring is under a tension and may deteriorate, causing trouble.
4. The automatic can not use blanks or reduced loads.
5. It has a poorer trigger pull than the revolver.
6. The magazine action requires a jacketed bullet which is not as good for practical use as a lead bullet.
7. The automatic pistol is more dangerous to handle, especially for inexperienced people, owing to the fact that after one shot it is always cocked and loaded.
8. It is not well adapted to reloading. It throws away the empty shells at each shot.
9. Many automatics eject empty cartridges toward the face, causing flinching.
10. It can not be fired from the hip as it throws cartridges into the shooter's face.
11. It throws out empty cases on the ground to remain as evidence.
12. It can not be fired from the pocket without jamming.
13. In some makes the hammer bites the hand or the slide strikes the hand and causes injury.

Disadvantages of the pistol

By far the most serious of all these disadvantages of the automatic pistol is its inability to use ammunition that is not up to the mark. For a weapon to use under any and all conditions where failure to function may be fatal, and where any and all kinds of ammunition may have to be used, the revolver is still far and away ahead of the automatic pistol, and is likely to remain so indefinitely. It is, therefore, still the choice of explorers and others to whom the possession of a hand arm in functioning condition is of paramount importance.

On the other hand, the automatic pistol is generally considered superior to the revolver for military use, where the ammunition supply is of known quality and spare parts are available.

The .45 Army automatic became extremely popular during the World War, and the experience with this arm at that time thoroughly justified the judgment of the Army authorities in adopting this as the service side arm for all branches of the Army.

For home defense use the small pocket automatic, which is usually hammerless, has the disadvantage of frequently lying for long periods of time with the magazine full of cartridges and the safety on. The magazine spring and mainspring may thus be kept under compression for perhaps years at a time. If at the same time the ammunition deteriorates from age, the result may be that the arm will not function when needed. Moreover, these small automatics always have safeties, which are an excellent thing for one who uses these guns enough to know all about how they function; but if one of these weapons becomes needed in an emergency by some member of the household who does not know much about using hand arms, it may very well occur, and has occurred, that the user was not familiar with the method of manipulating the safety and therefore could not fire the gun. These disadvantages are not shared by the revolver.

When it comes to readily understandable, to-the-point advice on handling a firearm, Jack O'-Connor stands in a class by himself. Here, in a selection from The Hunter's Shooting Guide *(1978), he offers a fairly detailed look at establishing intimacy with a handgun. His thoughts on flinching, the value of dry firing, and the value of getting started with a .22 are all of particular note.* **Jack O'Connor on getting started with the handgun**

BEGINNING WITH A HANDGUN

When the average American picks up a handgun and attempts to fire a shot he is about as much at home with it as he would be with a pair of chopsticks. Usually he couldn't hit the southern exposure of a northbound elephant at 30 yards. How come?

Possibly it's the influence of horse operas American kids have been seeing for the past 50 years. Unconsciously the impressionable lads absorb the technique of movie revolver shooting and imitate it. The heroes and likewise the villains grasp the pistol far over to the side. Before they cut a shot loose, they bring their revolvers back as far as the right ear. Then throw them forward in the general direction of what they plan to hit. Bang! go the revolvers. Down go the redskins, the villains, or whatever they are shooting at.

All this is excellent entertainment. The movements are fluid, the effect dramatic; but as a system of shooting a handgun it is enough to make a strong man wring his hands in anguish. The young moviegoers eat it up, not realizing that what they are seeing is not handgun shooting at all but instead a formal figure in a ballet. Watch a group of children playing cowboys and Indians some day and you'll find they handle their cap pistols just like the cowboys in the oat operas. Then when the time comes for them to shoot a real sure-enough handgun, they try their cap-pistol technique and can't hit anything. Often their beginning interest in handguns is killed because of their initial failures.

The hand-gun is the most difficult of all firearms to learn to shoot well

It is true that the handgun is the most difficult of all firearms to learn to shoot well, but if anyone starts right it isn't nearly as difficult as many believe. The lad who gets a suitable handgun, who starts using good form, and who practices will be shooting well before he knows it.

What sort of a handgun should the beginner select to start out with? The first fairly serious handgun shooting I ever did was with, of all things, a

.38 Special, but I wouldn't advise most beginners to tee off with a gun having that much blast and recoil. I do not think there is much argument but that the beginner's gun should be a .22. The little rimfire cartridge has many advantages. It is inexpensive, and can be obtained about anywhere in the world that ammunition is sold. But even more important is the fact that the .22 has a mild report and very little recoil. As we shall see, this is of prime importance, since flinching and yanking the trigger are the major reasons for poor handgun shooting.

What type should this .22 be, automatic or revolver? You have me there! For whatever the reason, I shoot somewhat better with a revolver than I do with an automatic. Possibly that's just one of my oddball notions, like my notion that I can do better shooting out in the field with a double-barrel shotgun than I can with a pump or automatic. Actually a very high percentage of crack handgun shots prefer the automatic because of its superiority in timed and rapid fire. Probably the revolver is somewhat *safer* because it is so much easier to see quickly if the weapon is loaded or not. The revolver also has the advantage of being able to handle .22 Shorts, Longs, or Long Rifle cartridges as the shooter chooses.

A high percentage of crack handgun shots prefer the automatic pistol

On the other hand, a .22 automatic with a fairly short barrel and good sights is an excellent supplementary weapon for the sportsman — short, flat, more convenient to carry than the bulkier revolver. The .22 automatic is a fine little weapon to pick up small game with, probably better than the revolver. Often I have seen grouse sit in a tree while a man with an automatic missed three or four times. The birds seem frightened less by the noise than they do by the movement of the shooter's thumb in the recocking of the revolver. Run-of-the-mine handgun shot though I am, I have eaten a lot of grouse and rabbits that I have plucked off with handguns. They tasted nice indeed. On one abortive sheep and elk hunt when my companions and I didn't get any real meat until the trip was almost over, we would have had to live on pancakes and oatmeal if one of my companions hadn't taken along a Colt Woodsman. As it was, we very largely subsisted on blue grouse and biscuits — and biscuits are a lot better with blue grouse than they are without. A rugged character I knew once walked 600 miles across the mountains and tundra of the subarctic in the dead of winter on snowshoes with a Hudson Bay blanket and a Smith & Wesson .22 target revolver. Mostly he ate ptarmigan and snowshoe rabbits, but he also killed a Dall sheep and four caribou with that little handgun.

The beginner should choose a handgun with adjustable sights

Whatever sort of a .22 our beginner selects, though, it should have adjustable sights. It is often said that no one can do an exact job of sighting in a rifle for another. It is even more true of a handgun. A revolver that is laying them in the middle of a 10-ring for one shooter may be clear out of the black for another. People see their sights differently. They hold differently. Because of different ways of holding, the handgun recoils differently and gives an entirely different point of impact. The same gun will shoot two different bullet weights to different points of impact and the same bullet at different velocities to different points of impact.

Nonadjustable sights are all right for close-range self-defense and military work, but the person who wants to do target shooting, who wants to knock over small game, or who wants to astonish the girl friend by making a tin can roll along the ground at a respectable distance wants a handgun sighted so precisely that he can hit a fairly small mark.

For target shooting, the common practice is to sight in a handgun with what is known as the "6 o'clock hold." Aim is taken at the bottom of the bulls eye, so that a thin white line can be seen between the top of the front sight and the bottom of the bull. The sights are then adjusted so that the bullet strikes in the center of the bull. Such a system is by no means universal even among competitive target shots. Some of the very best hold right into the bull—or sight in to put the bullet right where the top of the front sight rests. This is the way the plinker, tin-can roller, and small-game shooter should sight in, since obviously it would be fatal to have the bullet striking 3 inches high at 25 yards, let us say.

Tenseness is probably the principal enemy of precision

As in most shooting, tenseness on the part of the handgun shot is probably the principal enemy of precision. Take a look at a crack shot and he usually looks at ease, relaxed, almost sloppy. If he is going to be a topflight shooter he has to be, since tense muscles produce tremors and tremors make for poor shooting.

The first step then in learning to handle a handgun is to take an easy relaxed stance with the weight distributed evenly on both feet. Most good shots face half away from the target. I have seen many, though, who face the target and some who face away from the target at a right angle. The main thing is to feel comfortable and relaxed. The left hand can be put in the trousers pocket, hooked in the belt anywhere so it feels natural.

The handgun should be an extension of the arm

The handgun itself should be an extension of the arm, and a line drawn from the point of the shoulder to the V formed by the thumb and trigger finger should pass right through the sights. The arm, of course, should be straight, not bent.

The shooter should have a feeling of holding the gun with the pad of muscles at the base of his thumb and behind the large joint of his trigger finger while the gun rests on his fourth finger. If he does this and gets this feel, he should be grasping his handgun lightly but firmly. Depending on the size of his hand and length of his index finger, he will squeeze off his shot with the end of his index finger, somewhere between the last joint and the tip. He will *not* stick his whole finger through and squeeze with the second joint as the cowboys in the horse operas do. His object is to hit something and not simply to make a noise and look picturesque.

Holding a fairly heavy handgun out at the end of a straight arm is not the easiest or most natural thing in the world, and anyone who wants to become a fairly good handgun shot can well practice strengthening those muscles. He can do dry firing, of which more later, or he can hold a milk bottle at full length.

The ideal way to learn to shoot a handgun would be to go through a course of dry firing for a couple of weeks before buying any powder. Possibly that is asking too much, because beginners like noise and action. However, 75 percent of what can be learned by actual shooting can also be learned cheaper and easier by dry firing.

Most accurate handgun sights are of the Patridge type, with square notch in the rear sight and square blade front sight. With such sights elevation is controlled by seeing that the front sight is on the level with the rear sight and windage by seeing that the front sight is in the middle of the square cut of the rear sight — by seeing the same amount of light on each side of the front sight.

Good shotgun shots see the end of the barrel only vaguely. Instead they concentrate on the bird or clay target they are trying to hit. The handgun shot is exactly the opposite. If he is to hit much he must pay more attention to his sights than he does

Good shotgun shots see the end of the barrel only vaguely

to his target. Actually very high scores have been fired by turning the paper around and aligning the sights simply on the middle of the target. The bull's-eye would not be seen at all, yet in many cases scores would be better than the same shooter could fire by aiming at the bull! *It is absolutely fatal to let the target distract the shooter's attention from his sights!*

The beginner with the handgun is shocked and disillusioned when be discovers that he cannot hold his weapon still. Instead the doggoned front sight wiggles around in a manner to drive one nuts. Unless he is carefully coached or has read and followed some sort of elementary instructions like these, he almost always falls into the bad habit of trying to grab off a bull when the sights look just right. He thus gets into the habit of trigger jerking — and no trigger jerker can ever hit much with a handgun.

There is only one way to begin shooting a handgun

There is but one way for anyone to begin shooting a handgun and that is to keep the sights looking as good as possible and then to keep increasing pressure on the trigger until the gun goes off. Anyone who can get that through his noggin and who has enough will power to practice it is already a pretty good shot. *The wild shots come not because one cannot hold the gun steady but because of jerks and flinches.*

The handgun shooter must concentrate on his sight picture, squeeze easily and steadily, and forget when the gun is going off. If he does that he can rapidly become a pretty good handgun shot.

I am just a catch-as-catch-can handgun shot. There is absolutely but one way for me to do fairly well with any handgun — and that's it. When I begin to think about when the gun is going off, I am sunk. If I ever try to catch 10 as it rides by I am likewise sunk. I have *got* to let the gun go off by itself.

But what about genuinely good handgun shots? One told me that he knew just about when his gun was going off. Another told me he knew exactly when his gun was going off. Another assured me that he could hold his handgun rock-steady for a moment while he squeezed. But no matter what the hotshots say, the average shooter becomes pretty good only by being relaxed and comfortable, by paying more attention to his sight picture than he does to the target, and by squeezing and forgetting that his gun is ever going to go off. This business of steady holding takes care of itself, as the longer one practices, the more one shoots, the more nearly steady he can hold a handgun. He never will hold it absolutely steady and should not expect to.

The average shooter becomes good only by being relaxed

The man who starts right with a handgun and does not form a lot of bad habits he has to break is lucky indeed. The man who knows how to stand, who holds his handgun properly, and who has learned to relax, who knows the sight pictures is all important, and who has convinced himself that the way to shoot properly is to keep squeezing and let the hold take care of itself is already a better shot than the average casual plinker. Then with a moderate amount of practice, this person will soon become good.

To some people accurate shooting with a handgun becomes a genuine challenge simply because it is the most difficult of all shooting skills to master. The shotgun shooter can give quite a flinch and the spread of the pattern will cover up for him. Flinching is much more serious with a rifle, but the great weight and inertia of the rifle cut down the penalties for flinching and jerking the trigger, although at that they are serious enough. With the handgun, jerking and flinching are absolutely fatal.

With the handgun, jerking and flinching are absolutely fatal

Not long ago I was amusing myself by shooting from 50 yards at clay trap targets set up in a sandbank with a .44 Special. Of course, I missed a lot, but when I hit one I got a genuine thrill of achievement. Even greater was my feeling of satisfaction because I didn't ever miss one very far. Another time I had a Smith & Wesson K-22 with me on a big game hunt. One night we were on a jack camp, reduced to flour, butter, jam, and a few cans of vegetables. We had a 20-gauge shotgun along for grouse but that day we were afraid of the noise it would make since we had located two banks of rams which we planned to stalk in the morning. With .22 shorts I knocked over a half-dozen big tender and trusting blues. We cut them up, floured them, and fried them in deep fat. Never have I eaten a better meal. It put strength in my legs, ambition in my head, and next day my companion and I went up and got those two big rams. A little ability with a pistol or revolver comes in pretty handy at times.

I know of no type of shooting which lends itself any better to dry firing than the handgun. Anyone who wants to get good should do a lot of it. A miniature target on the wall of a room is all any-one needs. If he practices squeezing off dry shots at this for fifteen minutes a day, he'll be surprised at how much his scores will improve on the range.

A. L. A. Himmelwright discusses essentially the same subject that Jack O'Connor does in the previous selection, but his perspective is a quite different one. His in-depth look at pulling the trigger addresses in a timeless fashion one of the two most common reasons for inaccurate hand-gun shooting (flinching being the other one). Similarly, his thoughts on target practice, though written generations ago, remain just as valid today as they were when the ink was drying on the first print run of Pistol and Revolver Shooting *(1915), from which this selection is taken.*

A. L. A. Himmel-wright dis-cusses trigger pulling and target practice

HINTS TO BEGINNERS

FIRING

With the pistol or revolver in the right hand cock the hammer with the thumb, making sure that the trigger finger is free from the trigger and resting against the forward inner surface of the trigger guard. In cocking the piece have the barrel pointing upward. Then extend the arm upward and forward, so that when you assume your firing position the piece will point about twenty degrees above the bull's-eye. With your eyes fixed on the bull's-eye at VI o'clock inhale enough air to fill the lungs comfortably and lower the piece gradually until the line of the sights comes a short distance below the bull's-eye. At the same time gradually increase the pressure on the trigger directly backward, so that when the sights are pointing at the bull's-eye the hammer will fall.

Be careful not to pull the trigger with a jerk, but ease it off with a gentle squeeze, so as not disturb the arm. Accustom yourself not to close the eye when the hammer falls, but note carefully where the line of the sights actually points at the instant that the hammer falls. You will, no doubt, find it almost impossible to pull the trigger at the moment the sights are just right. The hammer will fall when the line of sights may point a little too high or too low, or to one side or the other of the bull's-eye; but patient practice will correct this, and in time you will be able to let off the arm at the right moment.

Pulling of the trigger is a very delicate operation

The pulling of the trigger is a very delicate operation; it is, in fact, the most important detail to master — the secret of pistol and revolver shooting. If the trigger is pulled suddenly, in the usual way, at the instant when the sights appear to be properly aligned, the aim is so seriously disturbed that a wild shot will result. To avoid this, the pressure on the trigger must always be steadily applied, and while the sights are in line with the bull's-eye. It is, of course, impossible to hold the arm absolutely still, and aim steadily at one point while the pressure is being applied to the trigger; but, in aiming, the unsteadiness of the shooter will cause the line of the sights to point above the bull's-eye, then below it, to one side of it, and then to the other, back and forth and around it. Each time the line of the sights passes over the bull's-eye the smallest possible increment of additional pressure is successively applied to the trigger until the piece is finally discharged at one of the moments that the sights are in correct alignment. Long and regular practice alone will give the necessary training of the senses and muscles to act in sufficient harmony to enable one to pull the trigger in this way at the right moment for a long series of shots. A "fine sympathy" must be established between the hand, the eye, and the brain, rendering them capable of instant cooperation.

A "fine sympathy" must be established between the hand, eye, and brain

After obtaining a fair idea of aiming, etc., watch carefully when the hammer falls, and note if it jars the piece and disturbs the aim. If not, you are holding the arm properly. If the aim is disturbed, you must grip the arm tighter or more loosely, or move your hand up or down on the handle, or otherwise change your method of holding the piece until your "hold" is such that you can

snap the hammer and the aim remain undisturbed. This aiming and snapping drill is largely
practised by expert shots indoors, when they do
not have the opportunity to practise regularly out-
of-doors.

TARGET PRACTICE

If your first actual shooting is done at the range of
a club, it is best to ask one of the members to
coach you until you get accustomed to the rules,
etc. A target will be assigned to you, and you will
repair to the firing point and load your arm. It is
well to let your coach fire the first shot or two, to
see if your piece is sighted approximately right. If
so, you are ready to begin shooting. If, after several shots, you are convinced that the bullet does
not strike where it should, the arm is not properly
sighted for you.

In adjusting the sights you will find it an advantage to remember a very simple rule: To correct the rear sight, move it in the same direction
as you would the shots on the target to correct
them, or move the front sight in the opposite
direction. Most target arms have the front sight
non-adjustable, and the rear sight adjustable for
both windage and elevation. A few arms have in-
terchangeable or adjustable front sights for elevation. Move the sights a little at a time, according
to the foregoing rules, until they are properly
aligned. A few ten-shot scores should then be fired

for record. As you become accustomed to the range, rules, etc., you will feel more at ease. This will inspire confidence, and your shooting will improve correspondingly.

Do not have your sights too fine. Fine sights are much more straining on the eyes, and have no advantage over moderately coarse sights. The rear sights as generally furnished are purposely made with very small notches, so as to enable individuals to make them any desired size.

Do not have your sights too fine

It is well to have the trigger pull at least ¼ of a pound greater than the minimum allowed by the rules. If much used, the pull sometimes wears lighter; and if there is little or no margin, you run the risk of having your arm disqualified when you wish to enter an important match.

Never use other ammunition in your arm than that for which it is chambered. A number of accidents and much difficulty have resulted from wrong ammunition. In the same caliber the actual diameter of the bullets frequently varies considerably, and a few shots, even if they should not prove dangerous, may lead the barrel, and thus cause much delay and annoyance. When a barrel is "leaded" from any cause it will become inaccurate. In such cases, particles of lead usually adhere to the inside of the barrel at or near the breech. A brass wire brush, of suitable size to fit the barrel, will generally remove it. When this fails, carefully remove all oil, cork up the opposite end of the barrel and fill it with mercury, letting the latter remain in the barrel until the lead is removed.

Occasionally the powder is accidentally omitted in loading a cartridge. When the primer explodes, the bullet may be driven partly through the barrel and remain in it. When this happens, whether from this cause or any other, always be careful to push the bullet out of the barrel before firing another shot. If the bullet is not removed, and another shot is fired, the barrel will be bulged and ruined. This may occur with a light gallery charge.

When shooting the .22-caliber long rifle cartridge, there will be an occasional misfire. In withdrawing the cartridge the bullet will stick in the barrel and the powder spill into the action. To prevent this, hold the barrel vertically, with the muzzle up, and withdraw the shell carefully. Then remove the bullet in the barrel with a cleaning rod; or extract bullet from a new cartridge, inserting the shell filled with powder into the chamber back of the bullet and fire it in the usual manner.

Do not use BB caps in any pistol that you value. They are loaded with a composition of fulminate of mercury in combination with other substances that cause rusting and the bullets have no lubrication. These caps will ruin a barrel in a very short time. The .22-caliber conical ball caps are loaded with black powder, and the bullets are lubricated, making this a much better cartridge; but it is best to adhere to the regular .22 ammunition for which the arm is chambered.

Never, under any circumstances, shoot at objects on the heads or in the hands of persons. There is always a possibility of something going wrong, and such risk to human life is unjustifiable, no matter how skilful you may be.

It is necessary to exercise extreme care in practising with the pocket revolver. Some persons delight in practising quick drawing from the pocket and firing one or more shots. This is dangerous work for the novice to attempt. Most of the pocket weapons are double action. If the finger is on the trigger and the arm catches in the pocket when drawing, a premature discharge is likely to result, which is always unpleasant and sometimes disastrous. Practice in drawing the revolver from the pocket or holster should always be begun with the arm unloaded. Only after a fair degree of skill is acquired should actual shooting be attempted. For quick drawing from the pocket the only double-action revolvers that are fairly safe to handle are the S. & W. Safety Hammerless, and the Colt "Double Action," which has a safety notch for the hammer to rest on.

Exercise extreme care in practising with the pocket revolver

Drawing a revolver from a holster is easier and much less dangerous than drawing it from the pocket. Larger and more practical arms are generally carried in holsters, and such arms should be single action in all cases. In practicing with a holster weapon, fasten the holster on the belt, and anchor the belt so that the holster will always be at the same relative position. The holster should be cut out so that the forefinger can be placed on the trigger in drawing. Always carry a loaded revolver with the hammer resting on an empty chamber or between two cartridges.

In the woods, or in localities where such shooting would not be likely to do any harm, it is good practice to shoot at a block of wood drifting down in the current of a swift-flowing stream, at a block of wood or a tin can swinging like a pendulum, from horseback at stationary and moving objects, and from a moving boat at similar objects. Such practice is largely indulged in by cowboys, ranchmen, and others in the western part of the United States. The shooting is generally rapid-fire work with heavy charges at short range, and is to be commended as being extremely practical.

Many reports of wonderful shooting are gross exaggerations

Many of the published reports of wonderful shooting are gross exaggerations. The prowess of the so-called "Gun Men" of New York and other large cities is greatly over-estimated. These criminals do not practice shooting with the fire arms they use but operate by stealth and intrigue which makes them dangerous. They are, in fact, very poor marksmen, few of them being able to hit an object the size of a man more than 15 or 20 feet away.

In shooting a long series of shots with black powder ammunition, when the rules allow it, the barrel should be cleaned and examined every six or ten shots, depending upon the clean-shooting qualities of the ammunition used. It is well to examine the shells, also, and note if the primers have been struck in the center. If not, then some of the mechanism is out of line, and the parts likely to have caused the trouble must be cleaned.

After securing good, reliable arms, stick to them. Much time and progress is frequently lost by buying and trying different arms, ammunition, etc. If in any of your shooting, you should get results that are peculiar and unsatisfactory, make it your business to find out the cause of the difficulty, and remedy it as soon as possible.

"Blazing away" a large quantity of ammunition carelessly and recklessly is absolutely valueless as practice, and is a waste of time. Give your whole attention to your work, and try your very best to place every shot in the center of the bull's-eye.

It is very important to keep a full, detailed record of all your shooting, for comparison, study, etc. A suitable book should be provided for this purpose. Do not fall into the habit of preserving only a few of the best scores; but make it a rule to keep a record of *every shot*, and figure out the average of each day's work. The more painstaking and systematic you are, the more rapid will be your progress. By careful, intelligent work, it is possible to become a fair shot in three or four months, and a first-rate shot in a year.

It is possible to become a first-rate shot in a year

Charles Askins, Jr., had a great deal of practical experience with handguns. They were an integral part of his years as a lawman, he taught their use to military recruits, and he was a top-level competitive shooter. In this piece, "The First Training," taken from Colonel Askins on Pistols & Revolvers *(1980), he looks at putting the proper foot forward (both figuratively and literally) when one starts out.*

THE FIRST TRAINING

Anyone can be a pistol shooter — and a good one — if he can master the trigger pull. That is, if he can mash the trigger at that precise instant when the sights are aligned perfectly on the mark he will be an overnight success. It does not matter whether he grips the gun perfectly, stands perfectly, holds his breath perfectly, and has made a perfect choice of firearm and caliber; all are subordinate to the squash on the trigger.

The great bugaboo to successful trigger manipulation is an overpowering prediliction on the part of the gunner to jerk the trigger and not press it evenly and softly. These flinches are uneven and violent and swing the muzzle wide of the mark. It is my contention that sooner or later some enterprising handgunner is going to find a way to jerk the trigger uniformly. When he does he is going to have the battle won! It takes literally years to achieve a smooth, even balanced trigger squeeze. The laddy-o who will finally stagger onto a system whereby he can make his shots hit dead center and do it with a consistent and uniform trigger yank will show all of us the way! This oracle hasn't bowed onto the stage as yet and until he does we must labor along with the only system we know. A long and hard course of sprouts which produces results slowly and grudgingly.

The trigger releases the hammer through, usually, the design of a simple sear. To force the trigger out of its notch in the hammer requires a force of, generally, about 3 to 4 pounds force. This pressure is applied by the index finger of the shooting hand. On the face of it nothing could appear more simple than to tighten the first finger just ever so slightly and thus set the hammer in motion. However, a number of factors are involved which complicate the equation.

To begin with the pistol weighs only 2½ pounds, and when a force of this magnitude is applied against the gun it is bound to move. If that force is applied suddenly and violently as when the trigger is jerked the movement of the piece is exaggerated. This is only one of the problems.

While the trigger is being pressed ever so delicately the shooter must keep the sights in precise alignment with the mark and this requires some doing. When the gun is extended to full arm's length from the body it moves, wobbles, trembles and gyrates. As a matter of fact it is never entirely still. The business then is terribly complicated by the necessity for keeping the sights trained, one with the other, and the both with the

At full arm's length, the handgun is never entirely still

bullseye, meanwhile struggling mightily to control the tendency of arm, hand and firearm to sway, and all the time essaying to press the trigger only during those brief intervals when the gun is bearing dead on.

To be a really first-rate marksman, with the ability to press on the trigger smoothly, evenly, and gently, meanwhile maintaining a proper sight picture, and all the time holding the pistol with such good control as to keep the sights in alignment and press away the last few ounces of force required to set off the hammer necessitates, at a very minimum of not less than two years of constant practice.

There are an infinite variety of skills in the pistol game

If this is discouraging let me remind you that there are an infinite variety of skills in the pistol game. A marksman may be a going-hell-for-leather shooter or he may be just a dub. And as a helter-skelter sort of handgunner maybe gets more fun out of the sport than the bucko who is determined to be nothing less than a champion. It all depends on the *aficion*.

A good trigger should not have a weight of more than 3 to 4 pounds and that one which is nearer the three-pound breaking point is the better. It must be absolutely motionless, that is, when force is placed against it there can be no perceptible movement. Not in the slightest. When the pressure of the trigger finger comes up to 3 pounds the sear should let go cleanly and abruptly, there can be no feeling of sponginess.

There must be a trigger stop so that the very instant the sear is released the trigger comes abruptly against its stop.

To manhandle a trigger the shooter grips the pistol with a very hard grasp, straightens his arms completely, locking both at the elbow, and then he lines the sights one with the other. The only reliable sights for the handgun are the patridge type, i.e. a one-eighth-inch post in front and a square notch behind. The post completely fills the notch and the very top of the front sight is held precisely where the gunner wants the bullet to strike.

The only reliable sights for the handgun are the patridge type

With the sights in good alignment the marksman maneuvers the front post into the very center of his target. As the sight touches this point he places a little pressure on the trigger. Not a great deal of force for if he adds all the 3 pounds needed to fire the gun it will be violently diverted. Only a little force is applied, if it could be measured it would probably not amount to more than three or four ounces. In doing this the pistol is moved off the mark. The gun is never really still and the marksman only puts pressure on the trigger during those all too brief periods when the sights hang dead over the target center.

Once the 4-oz of force is pressed against the trigger the shooter does not relax this force as the sights swing off the center. He holds this and as he carefully works the front post back into the center of the target once more he tightens another 3-4 ounces. Again the gun moves and as at first he holds his accumulated pressure and slowly and patiently swings the sights back to the target's middle again.

This is kept up, never relaxing the pressure on the trigger, being careful not to inadvertently increase it while the sight is off the center, and finally after maybe as many as a half-dozen tries — squeezing only when the sights are dead center, holding the pressure while they are wide of the target, he finally forces the pistol to fire. The hit will be a fairly good one. This may take a full minute, with some slow-pokes it requires two or three minutes; with the experts it uses up only 2 or 3 seconds. And yet the squeeze of the latter is quite as precise as that of the meticulous one. It is all a matter of practice.

There is a school which advocates that the marksman squeezes and squeezes and is never certain just when the gun is going to fire. This is a **The shooter must know his gun and his pull** bunch of hogwash. The shooter must know his gun and his pull so intimately as to be certain within a fraction of an ounce exactly when the sear will release. Don't ever put any stock in the joker who tells you "just squeeze when the sights are on and the gun will go off when it is dead center." Garbage!

If a pistol weighed 40 pounds and the trigger broke at only three, we could punish the trigger in quick time and get away with it. But, unfortunately, this isn't true. The handgun, even the heavy ones do not go more than 3 pounds and a trigger let-off of this weight is common. Because of these irrefutable facts the pressure has to be applied with a great deal of caution.

It is best to grip the gun with both hands. In target match shooting the rules require that only one hand be placed on the pistol but in practice the two-fisted hold is perfectly cricket. I believe in it. You can simply hold a lot steadier, overcome recoil faster and suffer less punishment with the two hands on the grip. I'd recommend you start this way.

The two-handed grip is best

Even tho' both fists are wrapped around the stock, the control hand is the right. It is this index finger which works against the trigger, while it may be OK to hold the pistol with both hands only the one finger sets off the charge. Lay it against the iron midway of the very end of the digit and the first joint. All the nerves come to an end here and this is the most sensitive part of the finger. To put only the tip against the trigger means that both of the joints must be bent quite abruptly. This makes possible the placement of the finger at right angles to the trigger — and in exact prolongation with the axis of the bore. These may seem like inconsequential details but they all help to shoot better.

The second hand, normally, the left, is wrapped around and over the right. The most of the pressure on the gun stock is exerted by the right hand; for all that the grasp of the left is plenty hard. A pistol, regardless of caliber, is never held lightly nor loosely. And the bigger the caliber the harder the pressure!

The pistol is fully extended to arm's length. Both arms that is. And to do this the marksman fully faces the mark. Not at any angle at all, but full-face. This then makes comfortable the full extension of both arms. The elbows are locked, the muscles at the shoulders which support the arms are locked and the body is supported and steadied by a separation of the feet of not less than 20 inches. Some shorties may not straddle out this much and some of the Jordans will separate the heel by a full yard. Every man is a law unto himself. There should be no tendency to lean backward at the hips to hold the gun in firing position and there seems little inducement to lean into the piece in anticipation of the recoil.

The one-handed shooter, the target man who fires the national match course, turns about 45 degrees from the target, separates his feet about the same distance, fully extends his hand, locking the elbow, and with head and body erect looks over the sights. Some one-handed shooters actually turn 90 degrees from the target and in this stance take up more of the recoil from the heavy kicking handguns. It has something to commend it. The only objection, as I have found it, is that the aiming eye must accept all the burden. The left plays a very secondary role since it is sort of around the corner as it were.

It is best when making a beginning to fire two-handed. The shooter progresses more rapidly and once he has attained a certain modicum of skill may experiment with the one-handed firing if he is interested. It most certainly is considerably more difficult and should be attempted only after a lot of shooting with both fists.

The new shooting game called "Practical Pistol Shooting," a training in which the gunner makes a fast draw and triggers off a series of shots in extremely short time periods at silhouette targets set up at comparatively short range, has seen the development of a slightly different shooting stance.

Many of the practical pistol shooters slightly advance the right foot toward the target, bend both knees slightly, fully straighten the left arm but permit a bend in the right at the elbow. This position is OK for fast shooting and altho' it would not do for deliberate slow fire it has been found quite satisfactory for the fast rapid fire. Some gunners push the gun forward with the right hand and pull backward with left. Others reverse this procedure. They believe it not only permits a steadier grasp but also tends to counteract the recoil.

As the pistol is pushed out from the body and as the arms straighten, the aiming eye picks up the sights. The front post is 1/8" in width from top to bottom and the rear notch is a few thousandths larger so that the post fits the rectangular opening with a bit of light to spare on either side of it. A great deal of care wants to be exercised to be doubly sure that ribbon of light is the same on either side. Just as meticulously the shooter wants to be careful the top of the front sight only comes even with the top of the back sight. Not even $\frac{1}{1000}$" below the top nor even half that much above. But precisely!

Too much accent cannot be placed on alignment of the sights

Too much accent cannot be placed on the alignment of the sights. It must be done perfectly. Our best pistol marksmen, shooters like Hershel Anderson and Bill Blankenship, do not focus the shooting eye on the target at all. They focus on the sights on the pistol and see the mark as a secondary sort of thing. This is because the alignment of the front and rear sights is so absolutely important.

As the front sight settles into the back notch, the marksman catches his breath. He does not suck air like a beached trout but simply locks his breath in his throat. If he breathes while he is aiming and squeezing the gun will bobble up and down and a decent let-off is impossible. Hold the breath but if you are so tardy with the shot that holding in becomes strained or painful then the pistol wants to be brought back to the raised pistol position, the air expelled, a rest taken and the whole sequence commenced anew.

Bullseye shooters frequently aim one place and expect to hit another. This is readily accomplished with an adjustable rear sight. The sights are pointed at the 6 o'clock point on the black but the bullet hits dead center. The advantage of this is that the front sight is iron and is usually blackened with a lamp to make it nonreflective and in this Stygian state shows up a lot more clearly against the white paper.

I do not like this system, it is better to sight the pistol to hit the middle of the mark. It does not matter whether the target is in the shape of a bullseye, the silhouette of man or animal, is a knothole, a floating chip in the creek, or a tin can, it is far more practical to zero the gun to hit where it is pointed.

At any rate, and before the first practice the handgun must be sighted in. This should be done at not more than 15 yards if the gunner is a rank beginner. Better that the sights be adjusted by an old hand but if no experienced shooter is available then the tyro should test the piece over a bench and essay the job himself. No pistol as it comes across the counter can be depended upon to be in zero. This is a chore for the new owner and it is extremely important. If he feels that he is not competent to bring the arm to a decent zero then he had better cast about for someone to help him.

When you read his work, you find yourself developing an affinity for William Reichenbach. Quaint phrases and outright quirkiness aside, he writes in an engaging and entertaining fashion. Better still, for the purposes of the present book, he makes good sense. Here, in a piece that comes from his little book Sixguns and Bullseyes *(1936), he takes a practical look at how handguns should*

William Reichenbach on how handguns should be held

be held. Thoughts on the matter have changed appreciably in recent decades, particularly in regard to using a two-handed grip as opposed to only one hand, but what Reichenbach has to say about comfort, feel, and fit is as applicable as ever.

HOLD

A baby, as we know, has little trouble finding the place where the milk grows. To find the proper hold for a Revolver is equally easy. Nobody but a perfect moron will pick the barrel-end as being just as convenient as the other extremity. But right there is where most people stop thinking and that's why we have so many people that can't shoot. There are 14 different ways of holding a soup-spoon, 6 ways of gripping a tomahawk and 431 ways of getting the goat of your mother-in-law, but there is only *one way* to hold the stock of a Revolver.

There is only *one* way to hold the stock of a revolver

"Why be so fussy?" will you say. My dear fellow, telling somebody what the correct hold is, is like an initiation into a Hindu-temple. I always get jittery when I undertake it and I shall go into my grave long before it is time. I have had more than one intelligent pupil who, getting along in jig-time, will suddenly neglect his hold. They all have a way of compressing their lips and putting the glint of stubbornness in their iris. Here I am, trying to convince the thickhead that his progress will stop at "80" or thereabouts. (Mind you, I am doing it for nothing.) And he had promised so faithfully not to branch out on his own until he got to his goal.

Well, in this Manual the pupil can't talk back! So listen brother: There is only *one* correct hold! Get it? Thank you!

First off, we must realize that holding the stock of a Revolver should entail no physical strain — the gun should feel natural. We have some apostles who jeer about "ladylike grip" and so on. Those birds, probably, never have shown anything in the way of fine shooting. Just don't pay any attention! You can please only one master and listening to a number of "know-it-alls" will only set you back. Alright, we place the stock between the middle finger and the ball of the thumb. Then we drape the other fingers lightly wherever they feel comfortable. Got that? Now place your thumb on the latch — and presto!

Mind you, just drape the fingers around the stock, and do *not* touch the stock with your fingertips at all.

The lower part of the trigger finger touches the frame and should steady it. The little finger, also with its lower portion, does the same further down the stock.

The action of the first two digits of the triggerfinger is being dealt with under the chapter entitled Squeeze.

No pressure in any part of your hand, mind you! That seems to be the whole secret of HOLD.

However, it may not be amiss to amplify this statement. There is a reason for everything, as you will see presently.

Suppose, we practice the thing a little —

Just a minute! Don't pick up the Revolver like that — Take your hand off the gun! Are you a right-hander? Alright, pick the gun up with your *left* hand and *fit* it to your right. The idea is to give your shooting hand every possible help. You need it!

A handgun is not a blackjack or a club that must be gripped tensely. Violence or noticeable pressures are oriented in the cylinder and barrel, not in your hand.

Let's analyze the situation! Not only for the sake of correct learning, but also as an aid in acquiring consistency. Your middle-finger has the function to support the weight of the gun. It is placed where the trigger-guard meets the grip.

The middle-finger has the function to support the weight of the gun

You recall that the other fingers were placed below, first the ring-and then the little finger. Only if you were very stubborn would you wish to change this order.

Alright! Now, these fingers touching the *front* of the grip, would tend to make the gun tilt downward. We don't want that! Here is where nature comes to our assistance. As you will observe, the ball of the thumb is still unemployed. How about it? Right! Place that against the back strap (The rear-edge of the grip) and — there we are.   No more tilting, what?

But, we can't have the thumb floating around idly. Lay it on the latch.

Contrary to the beginner's usual conception, the gun must be held lightly! Just firmly enough to take care of a little bit of recoil. This light hold is beneficial in many ways. It tires you less. The gun remains steadier. Your motions and reactions are less acute — If you can bring yourself to regard the Revolver as a delicate instrument, you have gained much.

How does it feel?

We agree that the weapon is supported by the middle-finger; in fact, it literally hangs on it. Close to the second joint and on the side of the middle-finger (i.e. the side nearer the thumb) is the point of support. On the revolver, the corresponding point is directly in the rear of the trigger guard. This point serves also as a fulcrum. The pressure exerted by the middle, ring and little finger towards the rear is opposed by the ball of the thumb. The *vertical* movement of the muzzle, caused by the working of the mechanism and recoil, is checked by the thumb resting on the cylinder latch and by the ball of the thumb. The *horizontal* movement of the muzzle is governed by the palm and the sides of the trigger-and little fingers, as mentioned before and again the thumb, by its strategic position on the cylinder latch, comes into passive function.

By now you will readily appreciate the importance of what I said previously. *Do not touch* the revolver grip *with your finger tips*! The slight pressure they exert against the left side of the stock, the amount of which you cannot control,

Do not touch the revolver grip with your finger tips!

will destroy the delicate state of balanced forces (opposing pressures) which you are seeking to establish and maintain until after the weapon is discharged.

Now, try to memorize the procedure and practice holding the gun in the *same* way *every* time. Get into the habit!

Get into the habit

I might as well whisper a secret in your ear. It is all-important that, once you have found the correct hold, you must take and maintain it in exactly the same manner, with every shot — today — tomorrow — next week — all your life. Don't shift around! You should have invisible callouses in certain places in your hand and the stock should have invisible grooves and bumps, through your method of taking the same hold all the time. I said "invisible." You don't apply any pressures and therefore should not get callouses and wear grooves into the stock. I just used a sort of metaphor.

Another, and probably better, way of expressing what I mean would be to imagine the stock covered with a delicate film which, upon first correct contact with your hand, would show the impression of all the little skin wrinkles and folds of your hand. This impression, we go on imagining, must not be disturbed and, each time we resume our hold, all these skin wrinkles and folds should match the first imprint.

Start slowly and pedantically — Do it right! Practice it! And by and by, the gun will slip into the same place automatically — and that's what we want!

II
POSITIONS FOR
HANDGUN SHOOTING

Stance or foot placement plays a prominent role in most pistol shots. Although there may be some occasions, primarily connected with hunting, when the shooter lies prone or uses some type of support to enhance steadiness, we primarily think of handgun shooting in terms of standing shots. For a long time, an angled stance with the shooting hand extended was considered de rigueur, but the obvious advantages of two hands when it comes to steadiness, and the development of the Weaver Stance, changed that. Here we get a sampling of more traditional approaches on the subject, offered by two great gun writers, along with current thinking as reflected in the U.S. Army's training procedures.

Two approaches to handgun shooting positions

●

William Reichenbach had a special way of tendering advice, doing so in a pithy, humor-laced fashion that is virtually irresistible. In this short treatment of stance, taken from Sixguns and Bullseyes (1936), he explains the long-accepted way of doing things when shooting with one hand.

William Reichenbach discusses stance

STANCE

Ah me, you will sigh, what do we want with "stance?" We don't aim to shoot with our feet. Do you know that one of our foremost revolver-experts who read my exposition on stance in the first "Elusive Ten," wrote me that he thought it important enough to apply it in practice? Well Sir, we deal with this thing called "stance" because it is imperative to our success, not because we want to fill valuable printing space.

Did you ever observe a man slightly under the weather giving a speech to the world at large? We are not concerned here with what he may have been blubbering, but didn't you see that his body was swaying back and forth? — There we have it! *His body swayed*! Now, if the man had only had three legs, he would have presented a steadier picture, regardless of how much friend alcohol were urging him to sway in the breeze. We, of course, are more dignified. We don't hold speeches — not at street corners. We are busy drinking in knowledge, not alcohol, knowledge about "Swaying."

We can begin by making a little experiment. Alright! Stand in the middle of the room and close your eyes. After a short while you will have the feeling as if you were swaying — you *are* swaying! You are *falling*! You feel that, if nature had only provided you with another leg, things would be much steadier. Right? That's the trouble with having only two legs. A horse can *sleep* on its feet. We humans can't even stand steadily when fully awake. This is not a philippica against nature's shortsightedness; it is an endeavor to impress upon you the fact of "body sway." The best shooter, be he as steady with his arm as possible, will sway. His gunmuzzle is carried across the bullseye, in unison with the sway of his body. He has acknowledged that and he has taken steps to minimize the evil by assuming a correct stance.

Suppose, you were to acknowledge this fact now, instead of later? It would save a lot of time.

Alright then: The body sways in the direction of your chest. Just stand with your feet about 14" apart, the toes facing the target. Raise your hand and point with a finger at the bull. You will see that the finger moves mostly up and down.

Now point your toes both to the left and have your right shoulder face the target. Your finger will now travel across the bull from left to right and vice versa.

This kind of sway would interfere with your shooting, what?

Your shot-groups would be distorted. Swaying in the direction of the line of fire, your groups would tend to spread unduly in a vertical line, and horizontally, of course, if your torso were swaying across the line of fire.

Obviously since we cannot eliminate swaying altogether, we must try to minimize it. If we were

to take a position somewhere between the two ex-
tremes just mentioned, it would be evident that
our finger could not travel as much in one direction as before. You would find, in fact, that your
finger — or, if you were holding a gun, the gunmuzzle — moves within a very restricted area,
vertically and horizontally, but not enough to do
much damage.

Following up our reasoning logically, we will
now consciously apply the principle of correct
stance:

The
principle
of correct
stance

1. Stand with feet close together, facing in a direction of about 45 degrees to the left of the
   line of fire.
2. Move left foot straight to the left, a distance
   of 10 to 14", more or less, to find a comfortable position.
3. Now raise the heel of your right foot, turn
   on the ball of your foot to the left, until you
   reach a position of comfort.

As agreed before, even now the body will sway,
namely in the direction which your chest is facing.
But since — for right-handers — your target is
over to the right your gunarm has to be swung in
the direction of the target, also to the right, in a
line between your chest and your shoulder. In
other words, we introduce a sort of half twist in
your torso and that is why the muzzle travel is so
greatly shortened.

We can further reduce the disturbance by plac-
ing our body-weight correctly on both feet. We

"toe-in," until we can feel pressure on the outer margin of each foot. We also distribute the weight equally on both feet and on each foot evenly between the ball and the outer edge and the heel. In short: We were born with full soles and we should use as much of the sole surface as possible. This should be a boon to people with flat feet, what?

I hope, I don't have to implore you not to dismiss the matter of stance as trivial. "Stance" is one of the seven fundamentals. Get into the spirit and practice "stancing." See that you spread your legs so that you feel comfortable. The spread is individual — There is no hard and fast rule about the matter of inches. The stance must be comfortable and theoretically correct. You see, the thing you want to avoid is: having any tension in any part of your anatomy and that includes your shoulders, arms, body, legs and feet.

Do not dismiss the matter of stance as trivial

Your left hand which you find to be hanging rather helplessly should not be cause for giving it any thought. It is best if you just put it in you pocket and forget it while your pistol is up.

Jeff Cooper is one of the leading handgun authorities of the twentieth century, and in this selection he provides a clear, succinct overview of the various positions for handgun shooters, along with some helpful hints on how to make them most effective when it comes to marksmanship. The piece originally appeared in Jack O'Connor's Complete Book of Shooting *(1965).*

Jeff Cooper's tips on position

GRIP, STANCE, AND POSITION

SHOOTING POSITIONS

The
Weaver
Stance

The Weaver Stance — If only one method of shooting is to be learned, it should be the Weaver Stance, invented by Jack Weaver, of Lancaster, California. It is basically a two-handed standing position, but not the fully erect, straight-armed position of the target range. The big difference is that the Weaver Stance is fast, while the other is deliberate. Jack had to defeat his share of quick-draw artists to prove it, but prove it he did. Tests have now shown that a master can keep all his shots on the international target at 25 meters, starting with the weapon holstered and safe, and including reaction time, *in one second per shot*. At three full seconds, which is the regular time allotted to Olympic competitors starting with the pistol ready in the hand, he can keep all his shots in the nine ring. The Weaver Stance may be used with deliberation, but it is essentially a position for fast shooting.

To assume the Weaver Stance, face square to the target, with the left foot leading just a little. The right arm is nearly straight, the left arm bent a little more as the left shoulder leads, and the head is sometimes bent slightly into the line of sight depending on the shooter's build. On shifting targets, the body is pivoted from the waist without disturbing the fixed relationship of arms and shoulders. This position is accurate, fast, and extremely versatile. It is the best position to use in about 80 percent of the situations in which a pistol is necessary.

After the Weaver Stance come two positions which call for about equal attention, the braced kneeling and the speed rock. They fulfill opposite needs, for kneeling provides 100-yard stability while the rock is a means of stopping a lethal adversary at arm's length.

Braced Kneeling Position — To assume the kneeling position, first place your feet so that your heels arc in line with the target. This may be done as the pistol is drawn. Then drop so that your right knee touches the ground and sit upon your right heel. In this position your left shoulder is more advanced than in the Weaver Stance, so your left arm is more sharply bent as it supports your right hand. The bent elbow then rests easily upon the left knee, left elbow, and left hand all in the same vertical plane. The position is rock-solid and permits a rifle-like shot from an unready condition in about three seconds. Successive shots of course may be delivered with equal accuracy and greater speed. This position is of more use to the beginner than to the expert, for given equal time, the expert can shoot like a machine rest from the Weaver Stance. However, I recommend it highly for recruit training as it builds confidence in the beginner.

The braced kneeling position is of more use to the beginner

Speed Rock Position — This is the gunslinger's position, so called because it is the fastest way to get off a shot and because most practitioners rock the body slightly backward by bending the knees in order to start the barrel up toward level even before the weapon clears leather. In the rock — as used by a man (not a blank-shooter) who must hit a target — the grip is naturally one-handed, but the wrist and forearm are solidly locked. The pistol is pointed at belt level and fired as it lines up. This is a technique that calls for much practice and one that, to my knowledge, is never officially taught. Its speed advantage is perhaps a half second over the Weaver Stance, and its accuracy potential is limited to large targets at 20 feet or less, but it has saved lives. For the policeman who makes a traffic stop and is greeted by unexpected gunfire at 10 feet it is a most comforting skill to acquire.

The speed rock position is accurate only up to about 20 feet

F.B.I. Crouch — Related to the rock, but less useful, are the F.B.I. crouch and the so-called "lock-on." In these the pistol is drawn and pointed with some deliberation, but not from higher than diaphragm level. Good shooting may be done this way, but not as accurately as from the Weaver Stance and not much, if at all, faster. It is sometimes used in competition to split a difference against a specific antagonist whose abilities are known. It is also the only way that so-called hip shooting can be done with an improperly designed holster, as the speed rock works only from a speed holster. However, in practically all cases, if you aren't wearing a speed holster you had best settle for the Weaver Stance.

The so-called "lock-on"

Prone Position — There are many other shooting positions for the pistol which are interesting to experiment with, even though they may not be of much real use. For sighting-in or for an occasional ridge-top shot while hunting, the prone position is convenient. I have also used it in freestyle competition when the time allowance was ample. Prone is taken simply by lying full length on the ground and extending the basic two-hand grip straight forward. The pistol is supported firmly by the joined fingers of the left hand, with the little finger resting on the ground.

Care should be taken that no part of the weapon touches anything but the hands, and that the muscles of the right hand keep the same tension as when standing, otherwise the point of impact may be changed.

When using a bench rest the technique is the same as in prone except for that part of the body below the shoulders.

Sitting Position — The sitting position is not as useful to the pistolero as it is to the rifleman, since the accuracy differential between sitting and kneeling is pronounced with a rifle and negligible with a pistol, and the kneeling position is quickly and easily assumed while the sitting position is awkward to get into. Nevertheless, the sitting position is taught by the F.B.I, and has some usefulness in the field, especially when shooting from a forward slope across a canyon. To take it, sit down facing the target and assume the basic two-hand

The sitting position has some usefulness in the field

grip, with both arms straight. The torso is forced well forward so that, on level ground, the elbows are forward of the knees, which support the upper arms lying between them. This position is easily varied to suit different angles of elevation, from about 30 degrees downward to 45 degrees upward, which gives it its main usefulness. For firing horizontally from level ground it is not very practical; not as accurate as prone and hardly faster, and not as fast as kneeling and hardly more accurate.

If a backrest is available, such as the trunk of a tree, the braced sitting position may be taken, which is fully as accurate as prone or a bench rest. In this one the torso leans well back, somewhat as in a modern racing car, and the pistol hands are pressed between the knees, the feet being placed somewhat outboard for extra stability. From this you can shoot as well as the pistol can, but obviously conditions must be just right. It should be pointed out that a revolver fired from this position may scorch the trousers severely, as its flash gap is not clear of the shooter's legs.

Offhand is the official target shooter's position

Offhand Position — Offhand is the official target-shooter's position. Highly trained specialists can shoot brilliantly from it, but it is likely to discourage the ordinary man, since it is the least accurate sighted method of shooting a pistol. A conventional offhand position is taken by facing 30 to 45 degrees to the left of the direction of fire (depending upon the individual build), with the feet about a half pace apart, and extending the unsupported arm straight at the target. This traditional stance serves no useful purpose that I can see — though I used it unquestioningly for twenty years — and should be confined to traditional target shots and people with one arm.

A variation of offhand — the one-hand point — does have value in rough and tumble situations where one hand is necessary to hold on. Short-range unsighted fire is delivered in this manner when riding a horse, riding postilion on a motor-cycle, or hanging onto a bouncing jeep or a speedboat. The left hand holds the controls or a support, the body is placed as necessary, and the right arm is extended not quite fully, since a com-pletely extended arm lacks directional strength. The pistol is held about chin high, and the eyes focus on the target. The weapon appears as a ver-tical black bar just under the target, and the sights are not used. This is a wild way to use a pistol, but it works. Ray Chapman recently shot an X-pos-sible on combat targets from the rear seat of a speeding motorcycle over rough ground using this method.

The one-hand point

Barricade Position — Another position taught by the F.B.I. is the barricade position. To take it, shooter stands erect behind the barricade and places his inside hand flat on the edge a bit above shoulder height, allowing the web and thumb to extend outward. The pistol is held in the outside hand, which is placed in the web of the hand on the barricade. All of the body except the hands and half of the head remain behind cover. F.B.I. technique calls for the use of the right hand when shooting around the right side of things, and the left hand around the left.

However, with a little adjustment, the master hand can be used in either case with only a minute increase in exposure, and I suggest this for shooters who have extreme difficulty with the weak hand, rules or no rules.

The U.S. Army's Pistol Combat Training Techniques

From a contemporary perspective, one would assume that the U.S. Army would offer recruits what it considers the optimum in field training. This piece comes from a manual entitled Combat Training with Pistols, M9 and M11 *(2003). Although the text is somewhat dry, the information is eminently practical. Of course, it should be noted that the manual was written specifically with combat situations in mind, and proven combat shooting techniques may not always produce the most effective marksmanship in other circumstances.*

PISTOL MARKSMANSHIP TRAINING

The main use of the pistol is to engage an enemy at close range with quick, accurate fire. Accurate shooting results from knowing and correctly applying the elements of marksmanship. The elements of combat pistol marksmanship are:

- Grip.
- Aiming.
- Breath control.
- Trigger squeeze.

- Target engagement.
- Positions.

GRIP

A proper grip is one of the most important fundamentals of quick fire. The weapon must become
an extension of the hand and arm; it should replace the finger in pointing at an object. The firer
must apply a firm, uniform grip to the weapon.

One-Hand Grip — Hold the weapon in the nonfiring hand; form a V with the thumb and forefinger of the strong hand (firing hand). Place the
weapon in the V with the front and rear sights in
line with the firing arm. Wrap the lower three fingers around the pistol grip, putting equal pressure
with all three fingers to the rear. Allow the thumb
of the firing hand to rest alongside the weapon
without pressure. Grip the weapon tightly until
the hand begins to tremble; relax until the trem-
bling stops. At this point, the necessary pressure
for a proper grip has been applied. Place the
trigger finger on the trigger between the tip and
second joint so that it can be squeezed to the rear.
The trigger finger must work independently of
the remaining fingers. (Note: If any of the three
fingers on the grip are relaxed, the grip must be
reapplied.)

Two-Hand Grip — The two-hand grip allows the
firer to steady the firing hand and provide maximum support during firing. The nonfiring hand

Proper grip is one of the most impor- tant funda- mentals of quick fire

becomes a support mechanism for the firing hand by wrapping the fingers of the nonfiring hand around the firing hand. Two-hand grips are recommended for all pistol firing.

Fist Grip — Grip the weapon as with the one-hand grip. Firmly close the fingers of the nonfiring hand over the fingers of the firing hand, ensuring that the index finger from the nonfiring hand is between the middle finger of the firing hand and the trigger guard. Place the nonfiring thumb alongside the firing thumb.

Palm-Supported Grip — This grip is commonly called the cup and saucer grip. Grip the firing hand as with the one-hand grip. Place the nonfiring hand under the firing hand, wrapping the nonfiring fingers around the back of the firing hand. Place the nonfiring thumb over the middle finger of the firing hand.

Weaver Grip — Apply this grip the same as the fist grip. The only exception is that the nonfiring thumb is wrapped over the firing thumb.

Isometric Tension — The firer raises his arms to a firing position and applies isometric tension. This is commonly known as the push-pull method for maintaining weapon stability. Isometric tension is when the firer applies forward pressure with the firing hand and pulls rearward with the nonfiring hand with equal pressure. This creates an isometric force but never so much to cause the firer to tremble. This steadies the weapon and reduces barrel rise from recoil. The supporting arm is bent with the elbow pulled downward. The firing arm is fully extended with the elbow and wrist locked. The firer must experiment to find the right amount of isometric tension to apply. (Note: The firing hand should exert the same pressure as the nonfiring hand. If it does not, a missed target could result.)

Natural Point of Aim — The firer should check his grip for use of his natural point of aim. He grips the weapon and sights properly on a distant target. While maintaining his grip and stance, he closes his eyes for three to five seconds. He then opens his eyes and checks for proper sight picture. If the point of aim is disturbed, the firer adjusts his stance to compensate. If the sight alignment is disturbed, the firer adjusts his grip to compensate by removing the weapon from his hand and reapplying the grip. The firer repeats this process until the sight alignment and sight placement remain almost the same when he opens his eyes. With sufficient practice, this enables the firer to determine and use his natural point of aim, which is the most relaxed position for holding and firing the weapon.

The firer should determine his natural point of aim

AIMING

Aiming is sight alignment and sight placement.

Sight alignment is the centering of the front blade in the rear sight notch. The top of the front sight is level with the top of the rear sight and is in correct alignment with the eye. For correct sight alignment, the firer must center the front sight in the rear sight. He raises or lowers the top of the front sight so it is level with the top of the rear sight. Sight alignment is essential for accuracy because of the short sight radius of the pistol. For example, if a $\frac{1}{10}$-inch error is made in aligning the front sight in the rear sight, the firer's bullet will miss the point of aim by about 15 inches at a range of 25 meters. The $\frac{1}{10}$-inch error in sight alignment magnifies as the range increases — at 25 meters, it is magnified 150 times.

Sight placement is the positioning of the weapon's sights in relation to the target as seen by the firer when he aims the weapon. A correct sight picture consists of correct sight alignment with the front sight placed center mass of the target. The eye can focus on only one object at a time at different distances. Therefore, the last focus of the eye is always on the front sight. When the front sight is seen clearly, the rear sight and target will appear hazy. The firer can maintain correct sight alignment only through focusing on the front sight. His bullet will hit the target even if the sight picture is partly off center but still remains on the target. Therefore, sight alignment is more important than sight placement. Since it is impossible to hold the weapon completely still, the firer must apply trigger squeeze and maintain correct sight alignment while the weapon is moving in and around the center of the target. This natural movement of

The last focus of the eye is always on the front sight

the weapon is referred to as wobble area. The firer must strive to control the limits of the wobble area through proper grip, breath control, trigger squeeze, and positioning.

Focusing on the front sight while applying proper trigger squeeze will help the firer resist the urge to jerk the trigger and anticipate the moment the weapon will fire. Mastery of trigger squeeze and sight alignment requires practice. Trainers should use concurrent training stations or have fire ranges to enhance proficiency of marksmanship skills.

BREATH CONTROL

To attain accuracy, the firer must learn to hold his breath properly at any time during the breathing cycle. This must be done while aiming and squeezing the trigger. While the procedure is simple, it requires explanation, demonstration, and supervised practice. To hold his breath properly, the firer takes a breath, lets it out, then inhales normally, lets a little out until comfortable, holds, and then fires. It is difficult to maintain a steady position keeping the front sight at a precise aiming point while breathing. Therefore, the firer should be taught to inhale, then exhale normally, and hold his breath at the moment of the natural respiratory pause. (Breath control, firing at a single target.) The shot must then be fired before he feels any discomfort from not breathing. When multiple targets are presented, the firer must learn to hold his breath at any part of the breathing cycle. Breath control must be practiced during dry-fire exercises until it becomes a natural part of the firing process.

TRIGGER SQUEEZE

Improper trigger squeeze causes more misses

Improper trigger squeeze causes more misses than any other step of preparatory marksmanship. Poor shooting is caused by the aim being disturbed before the bullet leaves the barrel of the weapon. This is usually the result of the firer jerking the trigger or flinching. A slight off-center pressure of the trigger finger on the trigger can cause the weapon to move and disturb the firer's sight alignment. Flinching is an automatic human reflex caused by anticipating the recoil of the weapon. Jerking is an effort to fire the weapon at the precise time the sights align with the target.

Trigger squeeze is the independent movement of the trigger finger in applying increasing pressure on the trigger straight to the rear, without disturbing the sight alignment until the weapon fires. The trigger slack, or free play, is taken up first, and the squeeze is continued steadily until the hammer falls. If the trigger is squeezed properly, the firer will not know exactly when the hammer will fall; thus, he will not tend to flinch or heel, resulting in a bad shot. Novice firers must be trained to overcome the urge to anticipate recoil. Proper application of the fundamentals will lower this tendency.

To apply correct trigger squeeze, the trigger finger should contact the trigger between the tip of the finger and the second joint (without touching the weapon anywhere else). Where contact is made depends on the length of the firer's trigger finger. If pressure from the trigger finger is applied to the right side of the trigger or weapon, the strike of the bullet will be to the left. This is due to the normal hinge action of the fingers. When the fingers on the right hand are closed, as in gripping, they hinge or pivot to the left, thereby applying pressure to the left (with left-handed firers, this action is to the right). The firer must not apply pressure left or right but should increase finger pressure straight to the rear. Only the trigger finger should perform this action. Dry-fire training improves a firer's ability to move the trigger finger straight to the rear without cramping or increasing pressure on the hand grip.

Dry-fire training improves trigger squeeze

Follow-through is the continued effort of the firer to maintain sight alignment before, during, and after the round has fired. The firer must continue the rearward movement of the finger even after the round has been fired. Releasing the trigger too soon after the round has been fired results in an uncontrolled shot, causing a missed target.

The firer who is a good shot holds the sights of the weapon as nearly on the target center as possible and continues to squeeze the trigger with increasing pressure until the weapon fires.

The soldier who is a bad shot tries to "catch his target" as his sight alignment moves past the target and fires the weapon at that instant. This is called ambushing, which causes trigger jerk.

TARGET ENGAGEMENT

To engage a single target, the firer applies the method discussed in paragraph 2-4. When engaging multiple targets in combat, he engages the closest and most dangerous multiple target first and fires at it with two rounds. This is called controlled pairs. The firer then traverses and acquires the next target, aligns the sights in the center of mass, focuses on the front sight, applies trigger squeeze, and fires. He ensures his firing arm elbow and wrist are locked during all engagements. If he has missed the first target and has fired upon the second target, he shifts back to the first and engages it. Some problems in target engagement are as follows:

Controlled pairs

Recoil Anticipation — When a soldier first learns to shoot, he may begin to anticipate recoil. This reaction may cause him to tighten his muscles during or just before the hammer falls. He may fight the recoil by pushing the weapon downward in anticipating or reacting to its firing. In either case, the rounds will not hit the point of aim.

Trigger Jerk — Trigger jerk occurs when the soldier sees that he has acquired a good sight picture at center mass and "snaps" off a round before the good sight picture is lost. This may become a problem, especially when the soldier is learning to use a flash sight picture.

Heeling — Heeling is caused by a firer tightening the large muscle in the heel of the hand to keep from jerking the trigger. A firer who has had problems with jerking the trigger tries to correct the fault by tightening the bottom of the hand, which results in a heeled shot. Heeling causes the strike of the bullet to hit high on the firing hand side of the target. The firer can correct shooting errors by knowing and applying correct trigger squeeze.

POSITIONS

The qualification course is fired from a standing, kneeling, or crouch position. During qualification and combat firing, soldiers must practice all of the firing positions described below so they become natural movements. Though these positions seem natural, practice sessions must be conducted to ensure the habitual attainment of correct firing positions. Practice in assuming correct firing positions ensures that soldiers can quickly assume these positions without a conscious effort. Pistol marksmanship requires a soldier to rapidly apply all the fundamentals at dangerously close targets while under stress. Assuming a proper position to allow for a steady aim is critical to survival.

Pistol-Ready Position — In the pistol-ready position, hold the weapon in the one-hand grip. Hold the upper arm close to the body and the forearm at about a 45-degree angle. Point the weapon toward target center as you move forward.

Standing Position without Support — Face the target. Place feet a comfortable distance apart, about shoulder width. Extend the firing arm and attain a two-hand grip. The wrist and elbow of the firing arm are locked and pointed toward target center. Keep the body straight with the shoulders slightly forward of the buttocks.

Kneeling Position — In the kneeling position, ground only your firing-side knee as the main support. Vertically place your firing-side foot, used as the main support, under your buttocks. Rest your body weight on the heel and toes. Rest your non-firing arm just above the elbow on the knee not used as the main body support. Use the two-handed grip for firing. Extend the firing arm, and lock the firing-arm elbow and wrist to ensure solid arm control.

Crouch Position — Use the crouch position when surprise targets are engaged at close range. Place the body in a forward crouch (boxer's stance) with the knees bent slightly and trunk bent forward from the hips to give faster recovery from recoil. Place the feet naturally in a position that allows another step toward the target. Extend the weapon straight toward the target, and lock the wrist and elbow of the firing arm. It is important to consistently train with this position, since the body will automatically crouch under conditions of stress such as combat. It is also a faster position from which to change direction of fire.

Prone Position — Lie flat on the ground, facing the target. Extend your arms in front with the firing arm locked. (Your arms may have to be slightly unlocked for firing at high targets.) Rest the butt of the weapon on the ground for single, well-aimed shots. Wrap the fingers of the nonfiring hand around the fingers of the firing hand. Face forward. Keep your head down between your arms and behind the weapon as much as possible.

Standing Position with Support — Use available cover for support — for example, a tree or wall to stand behind. Stand behind a barricade with the firing side on line with the edge of the barricade. Place the knuckles of the nonfiring fist at eye level against the edge of the barricade. Lock the elbow and wrist of the firing arm. Move the foot on the nonfiring side forward until the toe of the boot touches the bottom of the barricade.

Kneeling Supported Position — Use available cover for support — for example, use a low wall, rocks, or vehicle. Place your firing-side knee on the ground. Bend the other knee and place the foot (nonfiring side) flat on the ground, pointing toward the target. Extend arms alongside and brace them against available cover. Lock the wrist and elbow of your firing arm. Place the nonfiring hand around the fist to support the firing arm. Rest the nonfiring arm just above the elbow on the nonfiring-side knee.

III
STRIVING
FOR ACCURACY

A variety of considerations enter into the accuracy equation. These include problems with stance or trigger squeeze, the heretofore unrecognized matter of which eye is dominant, improper technique, lack of practice, and use of a handgun unsuited to the shooter. Yet every shooter wishes to improve his shooting; that is why we constantly strive to improve our marksmanship. Here we have glimpses of a number of factors the serious shooter needs to contemplate as he works on his shooting form.

●

Sound journalist that he unquestionably was, Jack O'Connor knew to turn to others more expert than he when the occasion demanded such an approach. That is precisely what he does here: he takes wisdom from first-rate handgunners he knew and distills it into readable, reliable coverage. The material comes from his Sportsman's Arms and Ammunition Manual *(1952).*

Jack O'Connor discusses expert pistol shooting

EXPERT HANDGUN SHOOTING

The Experts Know How to Handle Handguns
— Here are all the Tricks of Their Trade

Few will dispute the fact that the handgun is the most difficult of all weapons to shoot well; also that, once sufficient skill is developed, using a handgun is one of the highest forms of shooting pleasure.

Every rifle-shooting fault is magnified with the handgun

Handgun shooting is just like offhand rifle shooting, although more so. Every rifle-shooting fault is enormously magnified with the handgun. The prone rifle shot can do a little flinching and cover it up pretty well because of his tight sling, heavy firearm, and steady position. If he tries to shoot offhand, wild shots make his flinch apparent. Nevertheless the rifle is both heavy and long-barreled, and what a nice flinch can do to a rifle shot is nothing compared with what it can do to a handgun shot.

Usually I am not too enthusiastic about the theory of training in one subject to become proficient in another. If a man wants to learn Spanish he should study Spanish, not Latin. And if he wants to think well and clearly on social and political subjects, he should study psychology and logic to find out how his mind works, and then do some plain and fancy contemplating on social and political subjects, instead of sharpening his wits through the study of dead languages and mathematics, as old-fashioned teachers used to advise.

However, supplementary shooting of the handgun is one of the finest of all ways to keep a rifleman on the beam, to perfect his trigger control, to steady his hold, to sharpen his sighting. The unsteady one-hand hold, the short sight radius, the light weight of the handgun — all make for mistakes that prove fatal, though a rifleman could make the same mistake and score fairly well. As a consequence a good handgun shot is almost always a *very* good rifle shot, whereas the reverse is a long way from being true.

A good handgun shot is almost always a *very* good rifle shot

For years a friend of mine did a lot of handgun shooting. He almost never shot a rifle, however, because he was not a hunter. Then some friends talked him into buying a .30/06. Much to their astonishment this "beginner" started immediately to knock their ears down in offhand matches. Why? He had already mastered steady holding and trigger control with a vastly more difficult weapon.

I am not going into the selection of a handgun here, except to say that the smart thing to do is to start with a .22 because the ammunition is inexpensive and its light report and relatively gentle recoil are not likely to bother the novice. The smart thing also is to get as good a weapon as one can afford. I have always liked the feel and heft of the revolver, but most .22 target sharks use automatics and there is no doubt that the short-barreled, light automatics like the little Colt Woods-

Start with a .22

man with the 4½-in. barrel are sweet to pack around for plinking and general small-game shooting.

Form in any sport is acquired only by thought and practice. Give a man a tennis racket or a golf club for the first time and he will pick it up all wrong. His stance will be terrible. For the most part there is nothing "natural" about good form.

There is nothing "natural" about good form

Likewise, the man who first picks up a handgun will do everything wrong. He will grasp it as if it were a dagger that he was about to sink in someone's back. He will hold it with a bent arm. He will waver and wobble the trigger.

All of which reminds me of a story. Back in my boyhood, a couple of Western ranchers had a falling out over a stolen calf and decided to go a-gunning for each other. They eventually met in a saloon. One walked in the front door just as the other, who had been powdering his nose, emerged from a rear door. They emptied their guns — and did no damage except to the bar mirror and the walls. Before they could reload, friends overpowered them. The law came in. They were fined, warned by the judge to keep the peace, and then turned loose.

They next met on the open range, and this time they started popping away at each other at about 80 yd. Again neither got a hit.

Then it struck one of them as being funny. "Joe," he called, "got an ax?"

"Not with me, you damned fool!" Joe replied.

"You go home and get yours and I'll get mine. We ain't a-doin' no good with these here six-shooters!"

Then they both began to laugh, and for years they told that story on each other. It turned out that somebody else had stolen the calf after all.

In getting the correct hold for a handgun, the first thing to remember is that it should be held at arm's length. A general tendency of beginners is to hold with a bent arm, but this is wrong. Try to think of the gun being held so that there is a straight line from the shoulder right through the sights to the target. **The handgun should be held at arm's length**

Furthermore, the gun should be held from the shoulder with no conscious tightening of the muscles of the arm. An attempt to get steadiness through stiffened arm muscles will produce an exactly opposite effect; arm and gun will vibrate every which way. Held from the shoulder, with the arm virtually limp, gun and arm will act as if one piece, and movement will tend to be up to control.

Left to himself, the beginner probably will *grasp* the gun rather than *hold* it. He'll clamp down on the grip as if it were the last dollar he had in the world. Instead, the handgun should be held firmly but lightly. The frame just back of the trigger guard should rest on the middle finger. (Think of it as being balanced there.) The thumb should extend high along the frame for steadiness, and also because the thumb in that position promotes *holding* rather than *grasping*, to use that term again.

Many beginners put too much index finger through the trigger guard

Many beginners (and also some darned good handgun shots) put too much index finger through the guard, so that the pad of flesh between the first and second joints contacts the trigger. This is O.K. for rifle shooting, where the feeling should be that one is simply gently tightening up with the whole hand. In handgun shooting, however, the sensitive ball of the fingertip should be employed to touch her off. If the index finger is too far through the guard, it often contacts the guard as well as the trigger, and part of the pressure is actually being put upon the guard. The trigger finger must remain free to complete the squeeze at the right time.

If your sole acquaintance with a handgun comes from having played cowboy and Indians with a cap pistol in your youth, this method of holding the handgun may seem awkward at first. However, that's equally true of a golf club or a tennis racket, and using the correct grip will soon seem as natural as rolling the eyes and uttering a gentle sigh when a lovely maiden comes floating by.

Most good handgun shots stand with their feet at a 45-degree angle

Most good handgun shots stand with their feet at about a 45-degree angle to the line of the arm. However, I have seen some very sharp characters face the target. Others continue the straight line of muzzle to shoulder through the other shoulder; in other words, they face away from the target at a right angle. But since the first method is the easiest and most natural, the beginner should form the habit of using it. Thrust the left hand in your pocket or rest it on your hip, so there is no temptation to wave it around and destroy balance.

Anyone taking up the handgun is appalled by the fact that the front sight wobbles and wibbles so. He hears talk about the champions' rocksteady holding, and feels like a very inferior fellow indeed.

Between us girls, I think that the "rock steady" handgun hold is purely relative — that actually there ain't no such thing. Holds range from very wobbly to fairly steady. Even a rifle resting with fore-end and butt on sandbags on a bench rest isn't "rock steady." The more a man practices, the more he develops the important muscles in hand, forearm, and shoulder, the steadier he can hold. He will never, however, become a machine rest. If he did, all the fun would be gone.

Stage fright, weak and untrained muscles, too much smoking, and not enough sleep will make the extended arm with the handgun wobble; but even at that the wild and unpredictable shots are caused, not by wobble but by flinching.

So if you're a beginner, don't worry too much about wobble. If the trigger is squeezed off smoothly and the sights remain more or less in line, the shot won't be too sour. Let me repeat: It is *flinching* — not wobble — that causes those wide shots. One way to convince yourself of that is

Don't worry about wobble

to shoot with a deliberate and exaggerated wobble; if you manage to keep the sights lined up, you'll find that you still do fairly well.

Now let us suppose that, instead of feeling strange, as it did at first, the orthodox grip has come to seem natural. You've learned to hold the handgun firmly yet not hard, because holding *hard* only accentuates the tendency to wobble. You're ready to try some dry firing — holding the handgun sights on a mark and squeezing off the shot with no disturbance of aim. (Dry firing, by the way, isn't going to hurt your handgun and every good shot does worlds of it.) If you can put up a 25-yd. pistol target in the backyard, well and good. Failing a backyard, paste a small bull on the window and go to it.

Shooting the handgun is a grand hobby

Shooting the handgun is a grand hobby, and one that is neither expensive nor troublesome to follow. The small-bore rifleman has to be loaded up with a long and heavy rifle, a heavy scope sight of high power, a spotting scope and stand, and what not. The pistol shot can put all his gear in a container no bigger than a brief case. One of the best small-bore shots I know has switched almost entirely to the handgun because he grew weary, he says, of taking care of so much rifle equipment.

A good man with a handgun can get a lot of game, if he has to, and a .22 pistol or revolver is an excellent supplementary weapon to take along on a big-game hunt. On a 30-day trip into the Rockies one time my companion carried a Colt Woodsman and used it very effectively. Almost every day we'd run into grouse of some sort on the trail and my pal had no trouble giving the whole camp an occasional feast of wild chicken. To the wilderness dweller a .22 handgun is almost a necessity for supplementing the diet with grouse and rabbit and, perhaps, porcupine.

I know some very good handgun shots who hunt varmints with their favorite weapons and who would rather knock over one jack rabbit with a .22 hollow point or a .38 Special at 75 yd. than a dozen with a rifle. One amazing character I know has killed *two* mountain lions with a handgun. Wait a minute and I'll make it worse. They had NOT been treed by dogs. In both cases he saw them when they were crossing mountain roads. He got one with a Colt Woodsman and the other with a little automatic for the .25 A.C.P.

To me, the most interesting thing about the handgun is the training it gives and the lessons it teaches the rifleman. Do you tighten up too much? Do you jerk the trigger? Do you have poor breathing habits? If you want to find out (and have a lot of fun doing it), try the handgun!

This selection comes from the Army Marksmanship Unit Pistol Training Guide *(1980). Poor trigger control, especially jerking or snatching the trigger (rather than pulling with a smooth, even motion, normally referred to as "squeezing"), can be a problem when shooting any type of firearm. However, shortcomings in this arena are magnified when working with handguns.*

Trigger control as taught by the U.S. Army

This straightforward text describes proven ways to optimize control of the trigger when firing a handgun.

TRIGGER CONTROL

GENERAL

Correct trigger control must be employed in conjunction with all other fundamentals of shooting. The physical act of applying pressure on the trigger to deliver an accurate shot may vary from individual to individual. Proper trigger control for each individual gradually assumes uniformity when the techniques of proper application are mastered. Many shooters, for example, maintain a degree of trigger control with a relatively light grip, while another shooter may use a very tight grip. Some shooters prefer to apply consistent trigger pressure at a rapid rate, while maintaining correct sight alignment. For another shooter, a slower, deliberate application may achieve the same results. An ever increasing number of shooters use the positive approach to trigger control, that is, once it is initiated, it becomes an uninterrupted, constantly increasing pressure until the weapon fires.

Many shooters use the positive approach to trigger control

Trigger control is of very great importance in producing an accurate shot. When the shooter exerts pressure on the trigger, he must do so in a manner that does not alter the sight alignment, or position of the pistol. Consequently, the shooter must be able to exert smooth, even pressure to the trigger. Furthermore, the trigger must be pressed in conjunction with maximum concentration, peak visual perception of sight alignment and minimum arc of movement.

In order to produce an accurate shot, the shooter must carry out many diverse, but related, actions. Fulfilling this action is compounded by the fact that the pistol is in some degree of motion throughout the period of sighting and aiming. The movement varies according to the stability of the shooter's stance. Consequently, the sight alignment deviates from the aiming area. Often it will move through the aiming area, pausing only for a short period of time in perfect alignment with the target. It is impossible to determine when, and for how long the properly aligned sights will stay in the center of the aiming area. This difficulty is aggravated further by the fact that the shooter is trying to execute coordinated actions when reflex action seeks to contradict them. Such a situation requires the development of conditioned reflexes, and improvement of coordination.

For an accurate shot, the shooter must carry out many diverse actions

The coordinated action of correct aiming, timely pressure on the trigger and the correct delivery of the shot is difficult and can be accomplished only by overcoming former uncoordinated reflexes or by acquiring new ones. Only through constant training and attention to accepted techniques can these new reflexes be acquired.

FACTORS PROVIDING FOR THE
CORRECT CONTROL OF THE TRIGGER

The pressure put on the trigger must come from independent movement of the trigger finger only. The gripping fingers and the thumb do not move or tighten. Keep the grip pressure constant. Align the sight, settle into your normal aiming area and exert positive, uninterrupted, increasing pressure, straight to the rear, until the hammer falls. You must not look for a perfect sight picture combination of rear sight-front sight-bull's eye. Instead, **Focus the eye on the front sight** focus your eye on the front sight, keeping it perfectly aligned in the rear sight notch. The blur of the out-of-focus target may move about slightly, but this movement is relatively unimportant. Any time the weapon is fired with good sight alignment within the normal arc of movement and it is a surprise shot, the shot will be a good one, and will hit the target within your ability to hold.

Trigger control has a series of actions that take place if a smooth release of the firing mechanism is accomplished.

Slack and Initial Pressure — Any free movement of the trigger, known as slack, has to be taken up prior to a light initial pressure. This action assures that the tolerances in the firing mechanism linkage are taken up and are in firm contact before positive trigger pressure is applied.

Initial pressure is an automatic, lightly applied pressure, approximately one-fourth or less of the total required to fire the weapon. This careful action is an aid in the positive pressure that will release the hammer quickly and smoothly.

In order to fire a controlled shot the shooter must learn to increase the pressure on the trigger positively, smoothly, gradually, and evenly. This does not mean, however, that the trigger must be pressed slowly. It must be pressed smoothly, without interruption, but the release of the trigger must take no more than 2 to 5 seconds. Numerous accurate rapid fire strings of five shots in ten seconds are fired in a cycle that allows only one second or less to employ the principals of correct trigger control.

Release of the trigger must take no more than 2 to 5 seconds

Smooth trigger action makes special demands on the trigger finger when pressing upon the trigger; its correct functioning determines to a great extent the quality of the shot. The most carefully attained sight alignment will be spoiled by the slightest error in the movement of the trigger finger.

Function of Proper Grip — In order for the index finger to be able to perform its function without spoiling the aim, it is first necessary to have the hand grasp the pistol correctly and create the proper support; permitting the trigger finger to overcome the trigger tension. The pistol grips must be grasped tightly but without any tremor. It is also necessary that the index finger clears the side of the stock. The movement of the index finger must be independent as it presses on the trigger, and also not cause any lateral change to the sight alignment.

Proper Placement of the Trigger Finger — It is necessary to apply pressure on the trigger with either the first bone section of the index finger, or with the first joint. The trigger must be pressed straight to the rear. If the finger presses the trigger to the side, undesirable things will happen. The weight of trigger pull will increase; because of additional friction on certain parts of the trigger mechanism an otherwise flawless trigger action will take on the characteristics of a poor trigger when side pressure is exerted on the trigger. Another consideration is the effect that side pressure has on sight alignment. Only slight pressure to the side is required to bring about an error in sight alignment. The prime cause of exerting pressure to the side is improper placement of the trigger finger.

The effect of side pressure on sight alignment

Ideal trigger finger placement may be modified to a degree by the requirement that the grip provide a natural alignment of the front and rear sights. The shooter frequently must make a compromise to overcome the undesirable effects of not being able to utilize each factor to full advantage.

Coordination — It must be emphasised that match shooting is successful only when all the control factors are consistently in coordination.

Ability to control the trigger smoothly is not sufficient in itself to produce an accurate shot. The trigger must be activated in conjunction with correct sight alignment, minimum arc of movement, and maximum undisturbed concentration. This might be called cadence, rhythm or timing. Under any name, it comes only to those who practice frequently. Occasional ability is not the answer to championship shooting. A three-gun aggregate requires 270 successful results. Consistent, exacting performance is enhanced by an ability to compensate automatically for errors. It is necessary during firing to press the trigger under varying conditions of pistol movement in conjunction with correct sight alignment. In order to apply coordinated pressure on the trigger, the shooter must wait for definite times when all factors and conditions are favorable. Frequently, it will be impossible to exercise maximum control. However, the shooter must never attempt to fire until he has completely settled into a minimum arc of movement.

Occasional ability is not the answer to championship shooting

APPLICATION OF TRIGGER PRESSURE

Positive Uninterrupted Trigger Pressure-Surprise Shot Method — is primarily the act of completing the firing of the shot once starting the application of trigger pressure. The shooter is committed to an unchanging rate of pressure, no speed up, no slowdown or stopping. The trigger pressure is of an uninterrupted nature because it is not applied initially unless conditions are settled and near perfect. If the perfect conditions deteriorate, the shooter should not fire, but bench the weapon, relax, replan, and start again.

In instances when the pistol is stable and steady, and the periods of minimum arc of movement are of longer duration, it is immaterial whether the release of the trigger is completed a second sooner or a second later. Anytime that the shot is fired with minimum arc of movement and the sights are in alignment, it will be a good shot. Therefore, when the shooter has established stable minimum arc of movement and sight alignment, he must immediately begin to press on the trigger, smoothly but positively, and straight to the rear without stopping, until a shot is produced. This method of controlling the trigger action will give the shooter a surprise break of the shot before any muscular reflex can disturb sight alignment.

A method of trigger control that is *not* recommended

Interrupted Application of Trigger Pressure or the "Point" Shooting Method — This is a method of trigger control not recommended, although used by some shooters. Some shooters think they can pick the trigger release time even after years of experience.

The shooter will align the sights and exert initial pressure on the trigger. He will then make every effort to hold the weapon motionless. During extremely brief moments of motionlessness, pressure is applied on the trigger. If the sight alignment changes and is not perfect, or the arc of movement of the weapon increases, the pressure on the trigger is halted and trigger tension maintained. When sight alignment is again perfect and movement diminishes, pressure on the trigger is resumed until the shot breaks, or after the slack in the trigger is taken up, Initial pressure is applied and the shot released by a single swift movement of the trigger finger when there is a decrease in the minimum arc of movement. In this case the presence of perfect sight alignment is not considered essential in initiating trigger action. Abrupt action in applying trigger pressure will disturb the existing sight alignment and other fundamental control factors are subordinated to a minimum arc of movement. The application of all other fundamentals is required regardless of whether or not they are optimum.

While applying positive trigger pressure straight to the rear, if any thought enters the shooter's mind to speed up or slow down this trigger pressure, it will result in the concentration on sight alignment being broken down.

The decision to increase the trigger pressure may result in a reflex action commonly known as anticipation and usually results in heeling the shot (The bullet strikes the target at approximately one o'clock). The recoil becomes more imminent and the brain will send a signal for the arm and hand muscles to react prematurely a split second before the shot is fired; resulting in frequent bad shots and low scores.

The reflex action known as anticipation

ERRORS MADE IN TRIGGER CONTROL
AND MEANS OF COMBATING THEM

The most serious and disrupting error made by the shooter is jerking — that is, the abrupt application of pressure on the trigger accompanied with muscular action of the hand and arm muscles.

If jerking was limited to abrupt pressure on the trigger, and the rapid displacement of the axis of the bore, it would cause only part of the results.

Jerking is usually accompanied by: the sharp straining of all the muscles in the arm and shoulder; the abrupt tightening of the hand on the grip; failure to press the trigger directly to the rear.

All of these factors, taken together, lead to a great shifting of the pistol to the aide and down and only a very poor shot can result.

Most frequently, jerking is observed in new shooters. Usually, because of a large arc of movement, favorable moments for producing a good shot are of very short duration.

The cause of trigger-jerking, is the practice of "snatching a ten-pointer," as the expression goes. The shooter tries to fire at the moment when the centered front sight, as it moves back and forth, passes under the lower edge of the bull's eye, or comes to a stop, for a brief time, near the center of the aiming area. Since these moments are fleeting the inexperienced shooter strives to exert all the necessary pressure on the trigger at that time. This rapid and abrupt trigger pressure is accompanied not only by the work of the muscles in the index finger, but also by the sympathetic action of a number of other muscles. The involuntary action of these muscles produces the "jerk," and the inaccurate shot that results. The young shooter, in anticipation of the recoil of the pistol and its loud noise, strains his muscles by flinching, to counteract the anticipated recoil. This is also known as heeling the shot.

Heeling the shot

Practice has shown that a young shooter must be warned sufficiently early in his training about the dangers of jerking the trigger and effective steps taken to instruct him in the correct technique of accurate shooting.

Difficulty in detecting errors in trigger control is frequently because the pistol shifted during recoil and errors are not recognized. The shooter has a more difficult time in evaluating his actions than a coach, and often does not realize that he is jerking the trigger, blinking his eyes, or straining his arm and shoulder muscles.

The easiest way to correct jerking in the young shooter is by the coaching of an experienced coach. A coach can more readily detect errors and correct habits that will produce poor trigger control. Frequently a shooter does not consider it necessary to prove conclusively whether or not they are jerking on the trigger. It is necessary, though, to know that if he does not get rid of the detrimental habit of jerking on the trigger, he will never succeed in achieving good results.

Signs of jerking are an increase in the size of the area of the shot group or shots off to the side which are not called there; chiefly to the left and down (for right handers). To correct this condition, the shooter must make a change in his training exercises, but in no instance must he stop them.

Dry-fire practice will enable the nervous system to rest from the recoil of the shot. By this practice some of the reflexes which are detrimental to firing (tensing of the arm in order to counteract the recoil, the straining of the muscles in expectation of the shot, blinking from the noise of the shot), are not being developed. They will, in fact, begin to decrease and may completely disappear.

Secondly, the shooter may continue regular-training, but occasionally he may practice "dry". This way, he will not lose the stability of this position, as well as the useful reflexes which the shooter has developed during the process of previous firings.

By aiming carefully and noting attentively everything that happens to the pistol when he presses on the trigger, the shooter will discover his errors and eliminate them. Training by means of ball and dummy and dry firing is of great benefit. It makes it possible to develop correctly and carefully the technique of pressing the trigger, and contributes to acquiring proper habits in controlling the trigger.

Dry-fire practice is of great benefit

When beginning to use dry firing the shooter must first overcome the desire to "grab" for a shot when the centered front sight is under the bull's eye. Despite the arc of movement the shooter must teach himself only to press smoothly on the trigger and to use the uninterrupted positive control method of trigger action. When the smooth control of the trigger again becomes habitual and he no longer has to devote special attention to it, he can again shoot live cartridges. After starting again to shoot live cartridges, the first training exercises should involve firing at a square of blank white paper, rather than at a target with a black aiming area. Simultaneously, the shooter must devote special attention to analyzing his performance, counteract the desire to jerk on the trigger, and be conscious of reacting incorrectly to the firing of a shot.

Another error committed by a shooter when controlling the trigger is "holding too long," that is, the drawn out action of pressing the trigger. **The "holding too long" error**

A consequence of holding too long is that the shooter does not have enough air to hold his breath, his eye becomes fatigued, and his visual acuity decreases. In addition, his stance loses part of its stability. Consequently, when he holds too long, the shooter presses on the trigger under unfavorable conditions.

Holding too long is a consequence of excessively slow and cautious pressure on the trigger. This is caused by the shooter's fear of producing a bad shot. Such indecisiveness and over-caution may be regarded as the opposite of jerking. Moreover, holding too long stems from the lack of coordination of movement which frequently occurs during those stages of training when the process of inhibition outweighs the process of stimulation.

The shooter cannot force himself to exert positive pressure on the trigger at the proper time

Simply stated, the shooter cannot force himself to exert positive pressure on the trigger at the proper time. One favorable moment after another goes past, and soon the chances for an accurate shot are gone. Naturally, the trigger control phase has been extended far beyond its effective duration. This situation frequently occurs after a period of dry-fire training exercises. The shooter loses the sense of the trigger's true weight when he fires for extended periods of time with a round in the chamber. When the trigger is released in a dry shot, the trigger seems to be rather light, but when the shooter switches to live rounds, the trigger weight seems to be considerably greater. He feels that he must exert greater effort to overcome this seemingly greater weight. Frequently, the shooter will blame his troubles on faulty adjustment of the trigger mechanism. Nothing is gained from such assumptions. More times than not, the shooter returns to normal trigger control since the root of the evil is lack of coordinated control and not trigger adjustment.

The restoration of coordination of movement, and the return to the correct balance between stimulation and inhibition is brought about primarily through systematic practice, match training and dry-fire exercises. It is precisely this method of training which develops the necessary coordination of the shooter's actions. When the shooter's movements become automatic, the trigger finger will operate in an unstrained manner, and the shot will break at the proper moment. It is important that each training session begin with a few dry-fire exercises. It has been demonstrated that such exercises are necessary for the development of accurate shooting. Such exercises may also be repeated after record shooting to restore equilibrium in the nervous processes.

Frequently, a shooter, when firing for record, is unable to fire a shot. After several unsuccessful tries, a loss of confidence will arise. Rather than risk a wild shot the shooter should unload the pistol, time permitting, and dry-fire a few shots. After restoring coordination of movement and regaining his confidence, the shooter Is far better prepared, both physically and mentally, for the delivery of an accurate shot. Firing the shot during the first few seconds after settling into a good hold will guarantee confidence.

We have considered the fundamental errors that arise in trigger control. Let us now consider a problem that is also closely related to trigger control — trigger adjustment.

The firing of an accurate shot depends to a great extent on the quality of the trigger adjustment. An incorrectly adjusted trigger aggravates the errors committed by the shooter as he exerts pressure on the trigger. Incorrect adjustments in- **Trigger adjustment** clude: excessive trigger weight; excessive long creep (movement of trigger); too light trigger weight; variable trigger weight.

The shooter should not try to overcome these difficulties with modification in his trigger control but take the problem and pistol to the armorer (gunsmith) for solution.

The U.S. Army on sight alignment

Taken from the same source as the previous selection, this piece deals with the critical matter of alignment. Although stellar marksmanship certainly involves hand-eye coordination, the accurate shooter aims rather than points. Here are data on how to align one's eyes with the handgun's sight for maximum effectiveness.

SIGHT ALIGNMENT

Sight alignment is the most important contribution to firing an accurate shot.

In order for the bullet to hit the center of the target, the shooter must aim the pistol and give the barrel a definite direction relative to the target.

In theory, accurate aiming is achieved when the shooter places in exact alignment, the rear sight with the top and ideas of the front sight, and holds them in alignment in the aiming area.

A requisite for correct aiming is the ability to maintain the relationship between the front and rear sights.

When aiming, the front sight is positioned in

the middle of the rear sight notch with an equal light space on each side. The horizontal top surface of the front sight is on the same level as the top horizontal surface of the rear sight notch.

RELATIONSHIP OF SIGHTS

It is necessary to be acutely aware of the relationship of the rear sight to the clearly defined front sight. Normal vision is such that the rear sight of the pistol will be as nearly in focus as the front sight. Some shooters may be able to see only the notch of the rear sight in sharp focus; the outer extremities may become slightly blurred.

Angular Shift Error — If the shooter does not observe correct aiming (maintaining the top surface of the centered front sight on a level with the top of the rear sight and equal light space on each side of the front sight), there will be few accurate shots. Most often, he locates the front sight in a different position in the rear notch. This accounts for a greater dispersion of shots on the target, since the bullets will deviate in the direction in which the front sight is positioned in the notch. This aiming error is known as angular shift error.

Angular shift error

Parallel Shift Error — If the hold (arc of movement) is deviating in near parallel error from the center of the aiming area, the shooter should know that these deflections will not lower the score to the extent of angular shift error. Therefore,   sight alignment is the most critical of the two. Thus, the accuracy of a shot depends mainly upon the shooter's ability to consistently maintain correct sight alignment. The main effort should be toward keeping your sights aligned. Holding the pistol perfectly still is desirable but it is not mandatory.

POINT OF FOCUS

Correct sight alignment must be thoroughly understood and practiced. It appears on the surface as a simple thing — this lining up of two objects, front and rear sights. The problem lies in the difficulty in maintaining these two sights in precise alignment while the shooter is maintaining a minimum arc of movement and pressing the trigger to cause the hammer to fall without disturbing sight alignment.

The solution is partly in focusing the eye on the front sight during the delivery of the shot.

It is imperative to maintain "front sight point of focus"

It is imperative to maintain "front sight point of focus" throughout the sighting and aiming of the pistol. The shooter must concentrate on maintaining the correct relationship between front and rear sight, and the point of focus must be on the front sight during the short period required to deliver the shot. If the focus is displaced forward, and the target is momentarily in clear focus, the ability of the shooter to achieve correct sight alignment is jeopardized for that moment. Frequently, this is the moment that the pistol fires. A controlled, accurate shot is impossible under these conditions.

When the eye is focused on the target the relatively small movement of the arm appears magnified. However, when the eye is correctly focused on the front sight this movement appears to have been reduced.

CONCENTRATION

If the sights are incorrectly aligned, the net result is an inaccurate shot. Carelessness in obtaining correct sight alignment can usually be traced to the shooter's failure to realize its importance. Many shooters will, in the initial phase of holding, line up the sights in a perfect manner. However, as the firing progresses and the shooter is concentrating on delivering the shot, he often loses correct sight alignment which he attained in the initial phase of his hold. Usually, when the shooter is unable to maintain a pin-point hold, his concentration on sight alignment wavers. An accurate shot is lost because the shooter is thinking of his arc of movement and not the perfection of sight alignment.

Another factor which contributes to the deterioration of sight alignment, is the feeling of anxiety which arises over the apparently stationary pressure on the trigger when attempting to fire. An im-

An inaccurate shot will result when sights are incorrectly aligned

pulse is generated to get more pressure on the trigger, so that the shot will be delivered. When the shooter thinks about increasing the trigger pressure, a degree of the intense concentration required to maintain correct sight alignment is lost. Even if trigger control and the hold are good, the net result will be a poor shot. Sight alignment must remain uppermost in the shooter's mind throughout the firing of the shot. Positive trigger pressure must be applied involuntarily. Consistently accurate shots are produced when the shooter maintains intense concentration on sight alignment during the application of trigger pressure, while experiencing a minimum arc of movement. Control of the shot is lessened in direct proportion to the loss of concentration on sight alignment.

For the average shooter, sustained concentration is probably limited to 3 to 6 seconds

The average, advanced shooter is probably limited in sustained concentration to a period of 3 to 6 seconds. This short space of time is the optimum period in which a controlled shot can be delivered. This concentration interval should be attained simultaneously with acquiring a minimum arc of movement, a point of focus, satisfactory sight alignment, and the involuntary starting of positive trigger pressure. If exact sight alignment is maintained, and the trigger pressure remains positive, the shot will break during the limited time the shooter is able to control his uninterrupted concentration. Result! A dead center hit on the target.

THE EYE

The principal difficulties which confront the shooter during aiming are determined to a great extent by the inherent characteristics of the eye and its work as an optical apparatus.

Recoil and the dread of recoil, even if subconscious, can be the bugbear of the handgun shooter. It may not figure prominently in the shooting of .22 pistols, but as the handgun's caliber moves up and the kick does likewise, the shooter faces an issue he must deal with. Charles Askins, Jr., addresses the matter in this selection taken from Colonel Askins on Pistols & Revolvers *(1980).*

Charles Askins, Jr. on recoil

KICKING HANDGUNS

If a man had 6 fingers on either hand he would be a better pistol shooter, maybe even seven digits would help the more. Too, if the wrist joint was not quite as flexible this would be a further assist. Recoil in the pistols is controlled by the fingers and the more of them the better. It might be for the really ambitious that a surgical graft of another finger or two would not be such a bad idea.

The uplift of the muzzle when the trigger is mashed is a most important item in the success of the shot for the gun commences recoil on the instant the propellant is sparked to fire. By the time the bullet quits the barrel the muzzle has raised and this is the final direction of the bullet. If the shooter's hand is weak and the grip ineffectual the muzzle upchuck will be considerable. What's even worse is that if it isn't constant from shot to shot the hits will be strung up and down on the target.

Target pistol shooters are compelled to bang off their rounds using only the one hand on the grip. This is in accordance with the rules. The new school of thought, exemplified by the silhouette marksmen, the hunting fraternity, and even the cops is that both hands should be gripped about the gun stock. It is the only smart way to go. To control the kick which has such an influential bearing on the goodness of the hit the more hands on the stock the better!

The two-hand grip is the way to go

The grip is second in importance only to the trigger let-off, the pistol is somewhat like the scattergun, it is never still and while we may get so good we can hold it almost rock steady we never entirely succeed. For this reason the pistol is a close relative of the shotgun, both are fired while in movement.

The trigger squeeze must be coordinated with that movement. The tighter, quieter and harder the grip the less wobble and the easier the squeeze. Any shooter almost regardless of who he may be can hold a gun steadier with two hands rather than with one.

And by the same token [any shooter] can control the recoil more effectively with the 2-fisted hold rather than the one. We have grown, these past two decades into a fraternity of big bore men. The twenty-two and the .38 used to be the popular shooting irons; with the old .45 Auto running a distinctly poor third. This isn't so today. The magnums are now edging forward most especially with the hunting clan. The .45 ACP from a distant 3rd choice is now clearly the gun preferred by the combat shooters. The cops stick to the thirty-eight not so much from choice but through the obstinancy of their city fathers.

The recoil of the magnums has a formidable bearing on accuracy, the more the kick the faster and the higher the barrel climbs and the more probability of a wide hit. To control this jump at least in some measure is the name of the game. One of the big factors in the successful manhandling of the big bores is the grasp on the stock.

Recoil has a formidable bearing on accuracy

Regrettably the stock makers have not really given much serious thought to the design of a grip for the 2-hand hold.

The stocks on all the big handguns are obsolescent because they are all designed for only the one hand. This will be corrected in time but right now we have to live with it, a complication that has got to be resolved is that the gunner wants a grip small enough to make a one-hand draw but afterward will then catch the grip with the left hand overlapping the right.

While the stock may be big enough to nicely contain the one hand there simply isn't room enough for the other. It overlaps the principal hand, usually the right, and while it is decidedly

important it is very much the accessory hand. Just
how this is going to be improved is a problem for
the stock designers. We'll hope they are working
on it.

Recoil is controlled so far as possible by a
tremendously hard grip. A force exerted by both
hands. A grip so strong that during the first few
months of practice the hands will tremble because
of the inordinately hard grasp. With time and
more firing the force put on the stock can be maintained and there will be no tremble. Unfortunately
we do not have a grip indicator with a handy dial
gauge to show the pressure to be 50 psi or whatever is proper. If we only had a neat little meter
which showed when the grip-pressure got up to
the proper limits the grasp could then be kept uniform. After that we'd all shoot better.

The wrist can be a weak link in the equation

Another weak link in the equation is the wrist,
it is a swivel and bends and gives under the force
of the up-turning muzzle. If, somehow, there was a
lock on that swivel what a boon it would be!

Since we can't snap that latch the gunner
wants to stiffen the wrist against the kick all he
possibly can. With the Big Berthas he must also
lock the elbows. This is easily done but a consci-
entious effort has to be made at least in the beginning for the recoil with calibers such as the .41
and the .44 magnums will break the elbow joint
unless the gunner is prepared to resist it.

There are two movements when the pistol is
fired. One direction is upward and the other and

secondary motion is angular and is away from the supporting hand. The palm of the hand provides the principal resistance to the kick while the fingers are secondary in their support. If the hand was better designed to hold the pistol there would be 10 fingers, 5 on a side and these when wrapped around the butt would dampen not only the up-chuck but also the tendency of the gun to kick to the left.

The fingers are not as strong as the palm and so these give way under the recoil. The muzzle not only rises but it kicks off in the direction of the fingers. That is to the left which sees a hit not only high but to the 9-10 o'clock point on the target. The addition of the left hand, wrapped as it is over the fingers of the right dampen this flip on the muzzle leftward.

That is one of the major advantages of firing any handgun with the 2-fisted grip. Some fine day when the shooting fathers become a little less hidebound there is no doubt in my mind that the rule will be revised to permit strictly bullseye shooters to compete with both hands on the gun. Scores will improve when this becomes reality.

Recoil is determined by the size and the weight of the bullet, by the weight of the powder charge and the poundage of the firearm. It follows that if a big ball of sizeable heft and backed by a strapping quantity of propellant is fired in a light frame gun there is going to be a lot of punishment! These are immutable laws and the guns and ammo de-

Recoil is determined by the size and weight of the bullet

signers are fully aware of them. It is for these reasons that handguns for the magnum calibers are designed around heavy frames. This is ordnance that weighs upwards of 44 ounces and some go as much as 60 ounces.

Since the recoil begins on the instant the powder commences to burn it is contended that one solution is to make the barrel shorter so that the ball and powder combo is more quickly free of the bore. The further contention being that the muzzle will not rise so high since it is free of the ball the more quickly. These theories are in fact partly true; the only fly in the ointment is that the shorter the barrel the lighter the gun and the greater the impact of the gases on the atmosphere at the muzzle.

This impact is one of the most violent phenomena in the whole recoil equation and must be given much weight in any consideration of the problem.

Hatcher on recoil velocity

Hatcher has this to say about recoil: "For example if we have a .38 Spl gun weighing two pounds and it fires a bullet which weighs 158 grains with a velocity of 860 fps, we would expect the gun to have a recoil velocity of 860 divided by the weight of the gun and multiplied by the weight of the bullet in pounds. As there are 7,000 grains in a pound, the bullet weighs $158/7000$ths of a pound, hence the recoil velocity would be 860 ÷ 2 x 158 ÷ 7000 which works out to 9.7 foot seconds.

"This is the velocity of recoil; but we are more

interested in the energy of recoil than we are in the velocity. The weight of the gun, combined with the velocity is what makes it hard to hold. Velocity in itself does not mean much without weight. Thus a tennis ball coming very fast is easy to stop; it has velocity but not much weight. A baseball has more weight and at the same velocity would obviously be much harder to stop.

"The energy if the recoil of a gun is equal to one half the mass of the gun times the square of the recoil velocity, or 54 ½ MV². The mass of the gun is the weight divided by the acceleration of gravity, or 2 pounds divided by 32.2; and the velocity squared is 9.7 multiplied by 9.7, or 94.09. Hence the recoil energy would be ½ of 2 ÷ 32.2 = 94.09, or 2.9 foot pounds.

The development of such improvements as the Mag-Na-Port, a design which incorporates ports or orifices in the top side of the barrel just back of the muzzle and which then jets the gases skyward before these same gases pass the muzzle is a monumental step in the right direction.

While the Mag-Na-Port is best adapted to revolvers it can be accomplished in the big automatics altho I am uncertain just how successfully since the ports in the barrel must necessarily be in perfect alignment with like ports in the slide.

Unfortunately, the large frame revolver, the common choice for the make up of the big magnum calibers, is sorry indeed for the control of heavy recoil. It is immutable that the deeper the frame on the revolver the harder it will kick. The

The large frame revolver is sorry indeed for the control of heavy recoil frame was designed during the last century and no improvements have been made since. The barrel stands some inches above the grip and because of this height the kick develops a turning motion which accentuates the punishment.

The big auto pistols are much better designed for heavy recoil

The big auto pistols are much better designed for heavy recoil because the barrel does not stand nearly so high above its support. This, beyond question, is one of the reasons the .45 ACP has crested in popularity among the combat shooters.

Ask the average handgunner and he will be certain the peewee .22 caliber has utterly no up-chuck at the business end. This is an illusion, it does develop recoil and while it is of little consequence to the garden-run user there are certain marksmen who give it full measure of serious concern. These are the fellows who shoot the Olympic rapid fire game.

This match firing requires a shot on each of 5 silhouettes in a time interval of 4 seconds. The shooter must commence with the pistol pointed toward the ground and upon the appearance of the targets which all swing into view simultaneously, has to aim and squeeze the trigger meanwhile swinging along to the next silhouette. It should be explained that so keen is the competition that it is not just a game of plugging each man-shaped target but an oblong 10-ring in the chest has to be punctured to insure a reasonable chance of being among the winners. Recoil, faint tho' it may be, is a factor. The Olympic aspirants all fire very special .22 Short cartridge, a round that is more accurate than the run of the mill but a selection, I suspect, more notable for its lightness of recoil.

Such accessories as the Bo-Mar heavy rib, an attachment for all big auto pistols and some few revolvers has integral sights both fore and aft but more especially is designed to add weight the entire length of the rib. Its prime purpose is to hold down muzzle flip.

The Clark heavy slide for the Model 1911 pistol accomplishes the same ends from a slightly different direction. Clark chops two slides in two and then welds the longer pieces together again. The finished slide is a full one-inch longer than standard. Besides the elongated slide there is a special barrel from Douglas to fit the elongated piece. While this precision job adds to the sighting radius, which God knows is appreciated on the .45 Auto, more particularly it does muchly appreciated things to the recoil.

Interestingly one of the very most accurate shooting arms in the handgun firmament is the Feinwerkbau air pistol. It is a .17 caliber and is shot at 10 meters. This pistol will shoot tighter groups than all save an exceedingly small number of the best Continental-tuned free pistols. Even tho the Feinwerkbau does not burn powder it too develops recoil.

There is a spring and a plunger with a piston attached and upon the release of the trigger this piston is driven forward compressing the air needed to give the .177 cal pellet some 450 fps velocity. The very movement of the piston is so disturbing it may be likened to the conventional kick of the powder-burning firearm.

To overcome this vibration the designers have struck on a novel system which on the release of the trigger also loosens the entire action of the gun which floats on horizontal rails for a fractional part of an inch. The weight of the barreled action magically compensates for the vibration of the rapidly moving piston and spring and thoroughly dampens these parts. The extraordinary design feature accounts in no small part for the phenomenal accuracy of this remarkable pistol.

Before the larger powder-burning handguns, and most especially the magnums are to be made truely accurate a similar development must come along. Recoilless artillery fires both frontward and backward. There is a moderate escape of gas rearward which reduces the recoil to negligible proportions. Fantastic tho' it may seem the big magnum handguns need much the same application.

Charles Askins, Jr. on hunting sights

This selection, also from Colonel Askins on Pistols & Revolvers *(1980), is included here because of the manner in which hunting sights can improve the sportsman's accuracy. Clearly, this piece has equal applicability to the next chapter of this primer, which focuses on hunting with handguns. Drawing on his vast wealth of experience, Charles Askins, Jr., weighs in on hunting*

*sights and gives the handgunner obvious reason
to consider them and their performance carefully.*

HUNTING SIGHTS

Probably the poorest sights on a hunting pistol are those of plain black iron. It does not much matter the color of the animal nor the background, his surroundings, the time of day, nor the position of the sun, those coal-black sights will show up poorly. I am a believer in a front post that is as star-spangled as the old fashioned barber pole. And if the rear notch is set in a bilious green, Navy brindle, or Polar bear white that is OK too.

The poorest sights are those of plain black iron

For strictly target panning the straight iron patridge out at the business end and a rear sight just as unprepossessing in appearance is alright but for game-taking this ain't so hot.

The facts are, in truth, a gold faced front post and a white inset rear may be easier to see and quicker to pick up but for gilt-edged accuracy this combo leaves quite a lot to be desired on the score of good precision. The contrasting colors don't do anything for visual acuity and this accounts for somewhat poorer performance but my contention has always been that the shooter can give up something here in favor of faster sight alignment.

There are two or three factors in the handgunning equation that are important. I have always contended the most important is the trigger mash but the sight picture is only a half-step behind.

No one can shoot any better than he can aim and when the shot gets beyond fifty yards the sight becomes quite critical. If it wasn't for the fact that the post in front and the notch behind were so close together it would not be such a problem but that proximity of one to the other makes alignment super critical!

The best target marksmen do not focus on the target but on the front post

The best of our target marksmen do not focus the aiming eye on the target at all but concentrate on the front post.

This, in effect, causes the bullseye to blur somewhat but it brings the sights into sharpest focus. This, they have found, accounts for closer hits and is conducive to better accuracy and performance.

This is alright for the bullseye panner but it is not recommended for the game shot. He has to keep his eye on the critter and simply move his sights into the line between shooter's eye and the living target. If there is something lost in the process so be it. The idea that the game is going to be a blur while the sights are in sharpest outline won't work when you are stalking whitetails!

Because ordinary pistol sights are a pair it is argued by some of the strategists that the best solution is a low-power scope sight. This dingus eliminates half the equation and in theory, at least, improves the prospects of a close hit. Too, the problem of fuzziness in either the rear notch or around the front post is negated. The crosshairs, if the scope is in adjustment, don't develop those funny aberrations that are all too common with the conventional sights.

Thompson/Center, the makers of the excellent line of Contender single-shot hunting handguns, has a new one that is yet to be proofed in the game fields. It is an optical sight which has no magnification, projects an illuminated crosshair into infinity, has windage and elevation adjustments, weighs 5 oz, is only 2¾" in length, and readily attaches to the Contender handgun. This accessory like the low-powered short-tube conventional scope, eliminates one of the two iron sights.

I am something less than enthusiastic about a glass sight on the belt gun. It violates, in my conception, the true utilization of the one-hand shooting iron. A handgun is meant to be short, handy, fast, and highly portable. When we hang an optical sight, however small, however compact, on the pistol it loses a lot of its utility. I want my hunting arm to be readily carried either at the hip or in a half-breed rig and the only way this can be comfortably done is to stick with the original sights. Maybe sights colored up like a Navajo at the annual corn dance but standard so far as size and shape are concerned are the answer.

I am less than enthusiastic about a glass sight on a belt gun

Sights have been wonderfully improved these past three decades, handguns except target models which were few, all had a rear notch machined into the top strap with a front that was usually a half-moon in configuration. Only a smallish handful of pocket models are so unhappily blessed today. A pistol because it is so short, with its abbreviated barrel and its sights all too close together needs the finest most precise kind of sights. And by this I mean sights that are not only adjustable but finely movable at that. The idea that all you need is a groove in the top of the frame and a semicircular blade in front is utterly wrong!

There was once a well established prejudice against any kind of an adjustable sight on a handgun. "These movable sights are too flimsy," was the consensus of opinion and it was most especially strong among that clan which took to the woods. The cops were just as adamant, they were double-damn certain that any kind of a movable sight was sure to be so weak it would not hold up on a service gun. This prejudice has now all but disappeared.

During those days when the only handguns that had adjustable sights were target models, Colt had a novel system whereby the rear sight was movable only laterally, and this permitted it to be gotten in zero from side to side; the front sight was adjustable for elevation. These were the crudest sights imaginable. Both had to be gotten in zero and then left strictly alone. The bucko who was so sanguine as to try to move his sights from distance to distance, as from 25 yards to 50, was soon hopelessly lost. Smith & Wesson had a fixed front sight and a rear that was adjustable for both deflection and elevation. The side-wise movement was accomplished by backing off on the left-hand screw and tightening on the right. This, believe it or not, was pretty definitive. The only point was that once you had the pistol in adjustment you left it alone!

The elevation was done with a single flimsy screw and once the zero had been found a second screw was supposed to lock the first in place. Sometimes it held but more often it worked loose under the impetus of the recoil and then the gunner was all at sea.

There was a manufacturer in San Francisco, named D. W. King who had a sight company called the King Gunsight, and he was very definitely ahead of his time. He developed a rear sight that was movable for both elevation and deflection and the adjustments were simple and uncomplicated and what was maybe even more important the lock on both would hold against the kick of the gun! Attached as an integral part of the rear sight was a raised ventilated rib. This was new and startling and handgun hunters did not know whether they wanted such a dingus or not. At the front end of this rib was front sight which was quite innovative too. It consisted of a one-eighth-inch red plastic post. King used to call his post "red ivory" but this was just advertising hocum, it was common plastic but it held its color very well. The notch behind was outlined in an inset white and between the two visibility was excellent. Just behind the red post and inset in the rib was a mirror made of chromium steel. This was supposed to pick up the light and reflect it on the post. This was another gimmick but it looked good and everyone who used the King sights and accompanying rib were happy with it.

Front sights on the hunting gun are placed from ½ inch to as much as a full inch above the axis of the bore, this because of the recoil which commences once the powder is sparked to flame. Actually these high standing sights are part blessing and part nuisance. They are quick and easy to find when a fast shot is needed but they are also terribly easy to cant. A canted shot is one that is fired when the sights are not truly perpendicular. A front sight canted to the left will pour the hit out in that direction. To my notion the advantages of the extra high front post outweigh its drawbacks. The old .45 Auto has a front sight, on the issue model, that is altogether too low and hard to see. When some enterprising pistolsmith adds a set of his high sights it is a decided improvement.

Sight design, the outline that is, has been muchly bettered here of late. Instead of the old half-moon configuration or something near it, we now have a ramp base with a post that slants away from the eye quite pleasingly. For the woods gun this can scarcely be improved. The base with its ramp effect, along with the post itself gets a front sight above the barrel far enough and high enough so it can be seen quickly and easily.

It used to be that bead sights were common on

the one-hand gun. If it was just plain vanilla the bead was made of black iron; if on the other hand, it was all jazzed up it would be of gold, or ivory or maybe canary yellow. The rear notch, U-bottomed to conform to the bead might be outlined in white. This was thought to be the *one plus ultra* of refinement and while maybe you never see a combo like that these days the truth is that out to 25 yards the big gold bead in front and the white outlined rear notch worked very well. It distinctly was not a target proposition and for shots on game beyond off-the-muzzle yardages it was pretty ineffectual but for all that it had its uses. Rear sights must stand up above the frame and be highly visible. The sight must be so prominent that it instantly catches and holds the eye once the pistol is lifted into the line between the man and his target. I like the Dan Wesson which has a sight that is $^{12}/_{32}$" in height; and the Ruger Blackhawk which stands $^{10}/_{32}$" in height. Along with this good size the rear face of the sight must be grooved, stippled or checkered to dampen sun glare.

Rear sights must stand up above the frame and be highly visible

A great failure of many manufacturers is to provide us with a rear notch that is too shallow. This is a fault of S&W sights and it has been that way for a very long time. Too, Smith sights usually have a notch that is too narrow so that the front post fits too snugly.

This lends itself to shots that plop to the left or right because the gunner cannot align the post with the good precision that is needed. A hunting

rear worth its salt should be not less than .09"
in depth and if it runs a full $\frac{1}{10}$-inch so much the
better.

Just as importantly, maybe even more critical,
is the fit of the front post in the rear notch. Far, far
too many sights as they come from the factory are
altogether too snug one with the other. There
should be a good ribbon of light on either side of
the front sight as it is held in alignment within the
rear notch. I'd reckon if these ribbons could be
measured that each would be not less than $\frac{1}{64}$-
inch. It is a fact that it is scarcely possible to have
too much light around the front post. The eye automatically centers the front sight in the rear anyway and because so often hunting conditions are
poor indeed on the score of good light the more
space between the sights the better.

The width of the front sight is the most critical part of the equation

The width of the front sight is a most critical
part of the equation. It used to be that all front
sights, almost regardless of the type of handgun,
had blades of $\frac{1}{10}$-inch. This was a standard and
even today, and especially on foreign imports you
will find front sights that are still this dimension.
This is poor indeed!

The first shooters to abandon the all-too-nar-
row front post were the target gunners. These
marksmen went to a $\frac{1}{8}$-inch sight and they have
clung to it ever since. Today, all our hunting revolvers and auto pistols have sights of this width.
It is very near the perfect choice.

One time I had a series of front sights made up
and these ran $\frac{1}{10}$", $\frac{1}{8}$", $\frac{1}{6}$", $\frac{1}{5}$" and one-quarter

inch in widths. I attached these sights, one after the other, to a Colt python with 6-inch barrel. The ammo was limited to Federal wadcutters .38 Spl. I shot 10 scores at 50 yards with each front sight. I commenced with the $\frac{1}{10}$" width and as the front posts grew broader I simply filed out the rear notch to compensate for the wider front.

The one-tenth-inch post shot the highest scores and made the best groups. I believe this indicated the popularity of this sight for lo these many years. The $\frac{1}{8}$" was next best. It shot scores almost on a par with the one-tenth but what was more revealing, I think, was that it was done with less eye strain and less hard work.

The $\frac{1}{6}$" front post was not so hot at 50 yards, it simply covered too much of the bullseye and scores and groups were enlarged. Where this sight really showed its worth was at 25 yards rapid fire. It was quick and easy to pick up, was plenty accurate enough for the 10-second stanza during which the shooter has to bang our 5 rounds, and generally indicated its real worth at the closer range.

The $\frac{1}{5}$", and $\frac{1}{4}$" blades were utterly no good at the long range. However at 25 yards both turned in very credible jobs.

If there were any lessons to be gotten from this test it was to pin down why the $\frac{1}{10}$" front post has had its adherents; and why the $\frac{1}{8}$" is the happy choice of virtually all today's handgunners. The latter is by long odds the better choice.

The pistol sights both front and rear, are in-

The $\frac{1}{8}$"-wide front sight is the choice of all of today's handgunners

tended to be viewed at a distance of 24 inches. This is the average length of arm of the shooting man and his gun when extended in firing position and presents the sights in a certain perspective.

When the gunner bends the shooting arm at the elbow, or rests both elbows on his knees as when firing two-fisted and in the sitting position; or when he tries to fire prone, the sights are immediately thrown out of the accustomed perspective. When this occurs accuracy suffers, the front sight commences to loom up too large, the back notch appears out of proportion, and alignment is poor. Unless the pistol and its sights can be kept extended at the usual 24-inch distance from the aiming eye trouble will ensue.

There is another side of this coin. With a lot of hunting guns sporting barrels of 8 ½" to 10 inches, the front sight gets to be like 30 to 34 inches from the aiming eye. If that post is only ⅛" in width it can look awfully skimpy and sometimes not too well defined. On all my handguns that I intend for serious hunting usage, I replace the standard post with another that measures 9/64-inch. On a brand new .45 Colt Contender with 10-inch bbl, I have swapped the regular front post for an even wider post. It goes 5/32-inch, and this looks good at the end of that ten-inch barrel, I'll tell you.

The only two worthwhile shooting positions in the game fields

In my opinion there are only two worthwhile shooting positions in the game fields; one is off-hand with a two-fisted hold; and the other is sitting with the one-hand grip, the arm rested over the right knee and the left hand behind the body and bracing it for greater steadiness. The business of taking up the sitting posture like a rifleman with the elbows on the knees and the gun gripped in two hands is for the birds. It places the sights too close to the eye and because both elbows are bent, is not steady at all. The prone position is ridiculous. The body is close to the ground, the head is thrown back so abruptly and the sights are too close to the aiming eye that it is futile.

Because of the inherent inaccuracy of the handgun at any very great distances plus the crudeness of the sights, shots at game want to be limited to close range. I recollect a fellow who should have known better who bragged about killing a pronghorn at 217 yards. The pistol was the AutoMag which for some reason was at that time rated as being just slightly more lethal than a nuclear weapon but in truth is far outdistanced at any such ridiculous yardages. The bullet in going 217 yards will fall 70 inches which means that either the gunner held over the back of the game and thus could not see it, or he simply jerked the trigger so hard the muzzle was pointed high when the gun fired. At any rate it was a contemptible thing to do and should never had been told in public.

A hunting handgun ought to be sighted in at 50 yards to hit point of aim. If chances are offered at 100 yards these should be passed up, this business of trying for a trophy at such yardages places the

A hunting handgun ought to be sighted in at 50 yards

shooter in a very questionable bracket. He is one of these jazbos who will freely risk a wounded and lost animal simply for the sake of trying the impossible. It is a reflection of good sportsmanship, stalking skill and woodsmanship to fetch the animal into the sights at 50 yards rather than to hazard the shot at distances beyond. There are a lot of jokers who will recite, chapter and verse, how with the .30 Herrett, or the .30-30 in the Contender, or the .44 Mag loaded with 26 grains of Bullseye have knocked off moose, caribou, elk and mule deer at distances so lengthy it took a long horseback ride just to get to the dead critter.

For those who have these tales to spin I can tell you 10-for-1 about the questionable sportsmen who tried the doubtful shot, crippled the game, and the trailing a failure left a fine animal to die miserably. The handgun is a hunting arm when it is used well within its limitations. And it does have decided capabilities in the game fields, keep the shots close and both gun and man will come off looking much better.

IV
HUNTING WITH THE HANDGUN

◈◈◈◈

Modern hunters enjoy a challenge. The days when putting meat on the table for the evening meal was the focal point of hunters belong to a world we have lost, and as a result, today's sportsmen have increasingly turned to approaches that demand the utmost from them in terms of stealth, woodsmanship, marksmanship, and similar qualities. That explains in large measure the exponential growth in the ranks of bow and black powder hunters, and there has been an appreciable upsurge in the numbers of handgun hunters as well. In this chapter, the increasingly popular sport of hunting with the handgun is presented as seen through the eyes of two real authorities: Jeff Cooper and Charles Askins, Sr.

●

Taken from Jack O'Connor's Complete Book of Shooting *(1965), this treatment by Jeff Cooper looks at the use of the handgun by the hunter in all types of hunting — from small game to big. Some sensible questions about certain types of*   **Jeff Cooper** *big game are raised, and the author suggests that the answer to the question of whether such animals are suitable for handgun hunting is a "qualified yes." Today that yes is no longer qualified, thanks to the development of better cartridges, the production of optical aids, and general technological advances.*

HUNTING WITH THE HANDGUN

Pistol hunting has been called a stunt, which it is, but hardly more so than any hunting which is not conducted strictly for meat. It has been called inhumane, but it is no more so than any other hunting if it is done with proper care. I have been told that, since the average hunter can't hit his rifle, he should not be encouraged to go around wounding things with a handgun. But the average hunter wounds plenty of game with his rifle. With a pistol he is more likely to miss, to the benefit of the game. There is no practical way to keep the incompetent bungler out of the woods, and he can foul things up as well with one weapon as with another.

A proper pistol is accurate and powerful enough for many types of hunting

Actually, a proper pistol is both accurate enough and powerful enough for a great many types of hunting. It will not do for tiny targets, long ranges, or pachyderms. Neither should it be used on lions, tigers, or the great bears. But there is plenty of hunting which does not fall into the foregoing categories, and a lot of it can provide excellent sport for the handgunner who is willing to work for it.

The three requisites for sportsmanlike pistol hunting are short range, proper equipment, and superlative marksmanship. A good range for a pistol is about 35 yards. Fifty yards is a long field shot; 80 is marginal; and 100 to 125 is strictly big league. Naturally this depends upon the size of the game — but the essence of handgun hunting is cover. The handgun is a "brush gun," and unless the cover is fairly thick it is not going to be the tool for the job. Certain game may be spotted from afar and then approached in cover — I'm thinking of the javelina — and this makes for good pistol situations, but the shot itself must always be a close one.

This range limitation is not, however, as serious as it might look. We do a lot of talking about those elegant 300-, 400-, and 500-yard shots but, if we're honest, we know they are exceptional. Most game is engaged at under 50 yards. At that distance an expert field shot with a good pistol can hit within 3 inches of his point of aim even under pretty adverse conditions. This will anchor a lot of game. On a recent prowl into the backwoods of Guerrero, one of Mexico's wilder regions, I had a rifle, a shotgun, and a pistol available. In seven weeks' time I fired the rifle three times, the shotgun seven times, and the pistol seventy-two times. This was thick country, and the largest game was small deer, a perfect setup for my old Super .38

The requisites are short range, proper equipment, and superlative marksmanship and hollow-point ammunition. A .22 Jet would have been even better for the rabbits, birds, iguanas and pigs which constituted the main targets, but I needed something to serve a defensive mission as well, and I appreciated my *cuatro cargadores*.

Proper equipment means an adequate weapon, a carefully obtained zero, fine trigger action, and the right bullets

Proper equipment for the pistol hunter includes a weapon of adequate power and accuracy, a carefully obtained zero, a fine trigger action, and the right bullets. These matters are discussed in the sections on hunting arms, but I note them here again for emphasis. You should not blunder afield with a gaspipe under the impression that refinement is needed only on the target range. In the woods you stand to lose more than a high score.

Fine marksmanship is the ultimate key to handgun hunting, for while a mediocre rifle shot can do very well on a hunting trip, a mediocre pistol shot won't even get started. This corroborates the comparative efficiency of the two arms, for the master pistolero and the duffer with the rifle shoot just about in the same class — if you exclude such things as buck fever and mistaken targets, which will not bother the master. Theodore Roosevelt, who by his own admission was a very poor hand with a rifle, was a very successful hunter. I can't say how his hitting ability with a rifle would have compared to that of Ray Chapman with a pistol, who now has a string of seven clean, one-shot kills on big game to his credit.

As to standards, if a man can fire 135 x 150 on

the field course he is ready to go hunting. This is not too hard with a .22 but it's a chore with a full-house .44. Which is why pistolmen should stick to small game until they have attained quite a high gloss with their magnums.

SMALL GAME

Obviously small game is the most common objective of the handgun hunter. There is more of it, more time to shoot it, it's closer to home, and it's practical with a .22. Tree squirrels and rabbits, both cottontail and jack, are the most common targets, and they all provide most excellent sport as well as fine meat for the table. And they're not easy. One can easily be "skunked" in a whole day's hunting in good territory, especially if he tries only for head shots, as he should.

The marmot family makes excellent pistol targets. I consider marmots small game rather than "varmints" because I like to eat them, and edibility seems to be the difference. Marmots seem to call for a little more steam than a .22 Long Rifle provides, and will often make it down a hole when hit squarely with a service-type medium-caliber pistol bullet. Most of my experience with them comes from the goldens of the high Rockies, and I find that a .38 Super needs an expanding bullet to anchor them.

Any animal that is ordinarily treed with hounds is probably best taken with a pistol, as any man

Any animal treed with hounds is probably best taken with a pistol

who intends to follow a dog pack will do well to avoid the encumbrance of a long gun. The range is rarely over 30 feet, and at that distance a competent pistolero can hit a dime.

Treeable game in the U.S. includes the opossum, the raccoon, the bobcat, the cougar, and the lesser bears (*Euarctos*), and naturally the weapon used should be of adequate power for the game. Above all it must be loaded with proper ammunition. Brain shots are the most humane on a treed beast, but they are not always possible, and even the normally inoffensive black bear can work up a fair amount of justifiable indignation after being hazed to and fro across the countryside.

There are two major game animals which are often hunted with dogs but not into trees. These are the boar and the jaguar, and they are great prizes for the hand gunner. I confess to a certain reluctance to popping a treed quarry — the dim-witted possum, the charming and mischievous 'coon, the lithe and elegant cougar, or the quaint and comical bruin — but a burly hog or a massive, cattle-killing *tigre* is something else. Both tend to "come on" when the hunter shows up, and then comes the big moment for the pistol shot. The shot must be delivered coldly but very quickly. The range is short — too short — but the bullet must be placed with surgical precision, for you can't blast a furious, 300-pound beast to a standstill with pistol fire; you have to hit the central nervous system. Any man who has stopped a charging jaguar with his pistol rates a special feather in his war bonnet. This feat is to the pistol hunter as beating the drop is to the combat shot.

Varminting with a handgun is popular enough so that special weapons have been built for it; specifically the Remington XP-100 and the Ruger Hawkeye. The classical "varmints," in this country, seem to be woodchucks and crows, and hunting either with a pistol is a fairly specialized activity. As I said, I regard woodchucks as game, but I don't know about crows, as I have never eaten one. Both chucks and crows can get very cagey in regions where they are hunted extensively, and as a rule become essentially rifle targets, but in places where they are really pests they are fair game for a handgunner. A flat-shooting pistol is indicated, for distances can stretch out with either beast.

Rats are often found in large numbers in public dumps, and here is a really fine target for your .22. These repellant creatures are best jacklighted at night, and can provide a lot of tricky shooting in the course of an evening. Of course one checks the local ordinances first, but quite often a rat-shooter has the blessing rather than the disapproval of the city fathers.

Game birds are excellent pistol targets, but, except for the wild turkey, they are banned to the pistol shooter in the U.S. I have hunted ducks with a pistol in both Mexico and the Yukon, and believe me it isn't easy. One works to leeward along the shore, hoping to recover the birds as they wash up, and a slightly bobbing target flat on the water, with ripples intervening, calls for a fancy degree of elevation control. A hair high is an over, and a hair low is a short ricochet. You can try them on the wing, too, but don't expect much unless conditions are just right.

The king of the upland birds, for the handgunner, is the pheasant. You'll have to look pretty hard for a locality where it's legal, but taking ringnecks over dogs from the holster is a sporting enough activity for anyone. The rule is to keep your hand off your gun until the bird rises, and then to draw and track him as he goes out. A brace taken this way with a heavy pistol is somewhat more of an achievement than the same taken with an ounce and a half of number fours. A load of 1000 f/s or less is indicated, to avoid meat spoilage.

Taking turkeys with a pistol often offers good sport

Turkeys are the exception to the general prohibition on taking birds with a pistol, and often offer good sport. A fine account of a .38 Special on turkey may be found as the lead piece in the marvelous little book *Colt on the Trail*, published some thirty years ago by the Colt people as an encouragement to the field use of the sidearm.

MEDIUM-SIZED GAME

Of the medium-sized pistol quarries my favorite is the javelina of the Southwest and Latin America. Fast, excitable, diurnal, gregarious, and near-sighted, he is just right for the pistolero. When jumped, the flock is likely to explode in all directions, offering a series of difficult shots to several hunters at once. The .357 seems made to order for javelina.

However, when one thinks of American hunting one thinks of deer, and deer — whitetail, mule, or blacktail — are very satisfactory game for the handgunner. The best states are Alaska, Arizona, New Mexico, and Idaho; though Wyoming, Montana, and Florida are also good if you can get a positive ruling on pistol hunting out of their game departments.

Deer — whitetail, mule, or blacktail — are very satisfactory game for the handgunner

One of the really fine deer parks for the pistolero is the Kaibab plateau of Arizona, a state that specifies the .357 and the .44 (and now, presumably, the .41) as legal deer cartridges. The Kaibab is a high, rolling timberland and one of the world's most beautiful forests. It is inhabited by a carefully managed herd of big, handsome, well-fed mule deer that is hunted just hard enough to make it wary. The conifers and aspens provide enough cover for close shots without developing into a tangle, and each little draw has a jeep trail in its bed to permit easy hauling for your kill. You can camp out or hunt from a lodge, and packing and freezing facilities are only half an hour to the north on a paved highway. Altogether a fine spot, marred only by a one-to-a-customer limit that forces the handgunner to take the first thing offered rather than to wait for a trophy.

For when you hunt deer with a pistol you can't be very selective about your animal unless you are prepared to risk total failure. Considering that a handgun is three times as hard to hit with as a rifle, and has only one-third its range, one must regard any full-grown deer as a prize, and take a trophy rack as a gift of the gods.

The deer hunter works the same way with pistol or rifle, except that he simply avoids terrain that opens out too much. Setting 100 yards as his limit (remember, only an expert should take the field) he prowls the timbered ridges, glasses the edges of clearings, and waits at saddles if the woods get too full of other hunters. Particularly effective is an upwind course just below the crest of a main ridge, crossing the tributary ridges at right angles and searching the small bay at the head of each draw, where deer like to lie up in the middle of the day.

For hand-gunning deer, 100 yards should be the limit

Such matters are better covered in a book for deer hunters. The handgunner who hunts deer must simply remember to stick to close shots, to master his weapon, and to use the right ammunition; and he will do very well.

The deer cartridges are the .44 and the .41, though any big bore, properly loaded, will do the job up close. The trajectory of the magnums is their big advantage, for the hunter has enough problems without having to lob his shot at 75 yards.

BIG GAME

The question must eventually arise as to whether the pistol may properly be used on game larger than deer. I confess to a lack of first-hand experience in this area, but I think the best answer is a qualified yes. After all, it isn't so much the size of the target as the range at which it is shot. The .44, using the Norma bullet, will shoot right through both shoulders of a moose and out the other side. Not at 300 yards, but at pistol ranges. If the hunter insists on close shots, and passes up the foolish ones, he ought to be able to take fairly large animals with humane, one-shot kills. On big animals the .44 does not appear to deliver the instantaneous knockdown of a .30/06 on a deer, but for that matter few riflemen have ever seen a moose knocked off its feet by a rifle bullet either. As long as the quarry staggers and falls within 50 yards, the kill may be considered clean, and a .44 Magnum bullet, through the heart, will achieve this on animals quite a bit bigger than a deer. Thus I believe that elk and moose, together with the African antelope, may properly be taken with a handgun under special circumstances. By no means do I recommend this as a general pastime, but I hope I have made clear by now that pistol hunting is never a sport for the ordinary sportsman.

Since the pistol hunter is rather unusual to

Elk, moose, and the African antelope may properly be taken with a handgun under special circumstances

begin with, he has the advantage of being able to forget convention. Since he's not after a Boone and Crockett head anyway, he can branch out. There are a number of beasts which are not game animals in the strict sense, but which, in these days of diminished conventional hunting, may offer fine sport to men in search of the unusual. Particularly I have in mind the crocodilians — alligators, crocodiles, caimans and gavials. These are big, rough, not uncommon in the right regions, and can be dangerous. They are scorned by the riflemen as they lie in mesozoic sloth on the sandbar, but how about tackling a 20-footer with your .44?

Handgunning the crocodilians

Experts claim there is only one good place for your bullet, and that is in the center of the short neck directly from the side. This will anchor, while anything else will let the beast make it to the water. It ought to be feasible to spot downriver, then land and make an inshore approach to a point just at the edge of cover. Then, if you can hit a half dollar at whatever distance you can close to, a 240-grain steel-jacketed soft-point should net you enough leather to fill a shoe store.

And keep in mind that these latter-day dinosaurs come in several degrees of impressiveness. The king is the saltwater crocodile (*Crocodilus porosus*) of Oceania. Up to 10 yards long, agile and aggressive, and notably fond of human flesh, a prime *porusus*, taken with a pistol, would be a trophy of which any hunter should be proud.

TOP PISTOL TROPHIES

Just as the rifleman gleans the world for its best and finest trophies, the pistol hunter can endeavor to establish a set of grand prizes which could stand as testimony to the special qualities of the handgun as a sporting weapon. I don't feel that it would be right simply to duplicate the rifleman's list, for while it is technically possible to secure an argali, or a tiger, or a white bear, or even an elephant, with a handgun, it is not a sportsmanlike venture. I realize that sportsmanship is a matter of opinion, but in *my* opinion one can go too far in attempting to do a job with "an instrument singularly unsuited to the task," as Mark Twain said of a golf club. It may be that any pistol is unsuited to the pursuit of big game, but I don't believe this to be true. I think there is a compromise area, where rare, burly, beautiful, or dangerous animals are sought at short range under conditions that make them especially suitable as pistol targets. In preparing my own list of top pistol trophies I realized that I immediately pose a legal problem, for in many jurisdictions hunting with a handgun is not permitted. I do not suggest breaking the law, I simply suggest that laws, especially game laws, can be changed. You can't win at Indianapolis without exceeding the speed limit. Likewise you'll find it impossible to collect the grand prizes of the pistol without securing certain legal dispensations. This can probably be done.

Some rare, burly, beautiful, or dangerous animals can be hunted with the pistol at short range

Jeff
Cooper's
choices of
the top five
big game
animals for
the hand-
gunner

The following, then, is my choice of the royal five for the pistolero, listed by continents. Naturally all specimens should be prime examples of the species, as near to the record as possible.

Eurasia — For this area I'll pick the European wild boar (*Sus scrofa*), found from the Eastern Alps to the Tien Shan. He is a short-range target, rugged and quarrelsome, and he is quite capable of killing you. Taken with a pistol as you come up on the dogs, his 300 pounds must be stopped by the most careful use of the heavy handgun. Since most of his habitat is presently behind the Iron Curtain there are fairly difficult problems to be solved in getting at him. (Imagine trying to get a visa for your .45 auto!) But he has been imported into the U.S., so let's accept an immigrant, especially if he is outstandingly big and bellicose.

Africa — Here again the current political situation is so unstable that it's hard to say what the rules are or how they are enforced. In ex-English areas the pistol is probably still viewed with horror, but in the Portuguese colonies, east and west, people are more reasonable if they are approached politely. Skipping the giants and the traditional, I'll choose the gorilla. You'll need a museum permit to take him, but such can be had. If you threaten his group he will charge, and a charging gorilla is a fearful spectacle, to stand your ground with a handgun and flatten him at 15 feet is man's work.

North America — Again I will bypass the traditional, because the big bears are not humanely taken with a pistol. For a creature that is large, wary, noble in aspect, and a lover of the deepest forests where the range is short, I'll pick the Roosevelt elk (*Cervus canadensis occidentalis*). Bigger in body, darker in color, and with shorter but heavier antlers than the better known Rocky Mountain elk (*Cervus canadensis canadensis*), he is a beast of the dense, dank, rain forests of the Pacific Coast. He must be hunted with great skill, for you have to move in on him like a ghost to escape detection by his marvelously sensitive ears. And if you succeed in this, his massive body calls for very precise use of your .44 if you are to secure a clean kill. As of this writing, it is practically impossible to get permission to hunt the Roosevelt elk with a pistol, but this may change as handgun hunting becomes more respectable.

South America — There is no argument here, as the jaguar takes the prize. Not just any jaguar, but a really prime cat of 250 pounds or more. Such are hard to come by, and though Mexico's famed Enrique Job tells me that size is not a function of range, I feel the chances for a really massive *tigre* are best in the Mato Grosso and southward. Siemel, the spearman, has a photograph of one he took, the skin of which is so big that a tall man can just reach the ear when the hind legs touch the ground. This was Brazilian, but I understand that Paraguay, Bolivia, and Argentina claim some huge cats, too. Few English-speaking hunters penetrate the upper reaches of the Paraguay-Paraná river system, so there is not much written material available to us on the big cattle-killing jaguars, apart from rumor. This is one of the few remaining unspoiled hunting countries. Happily, there is no special problem about handgun hunting in Latin America, where the authorities seem more worried about rifles than pistols. If you can get a weapon permit at all, it is good for any sort of weapon.

Australia-Oceania — The warm waters of the Malay Archipelago and the north coast of Australia are the home of *porosus*, the aforementioned saltwater crocodile, and he is the last big prize. What with the Australians' anti-pistol bias, and the Indonesians and Malaysians perpetually on the brink of war, there are plenty of technical difficulties here. Also, *porosus* does not appear to be common, to the relief of the indigenous population. Here is a project for a man with a sea-going yacht, plenty of time, and a .44 Magnum.

Charles Askins, Sr. discusses hunting with the handgun

Charles Askins, Sr., did considerable hunting with handguns during the first half of the twentieth century, although Elmer Keith is rightly recognized as the gun writer who did the most to popularize this type of hunting. Here Askins offers his thoughts on the subject in an interesting and informative fashion. Some of the equipment-related limitations he addresses no longer exist, but his thoughts on approaches and choices of firearms retain their validity. This piece comes from The Pistol Shooter's Book *(1953).*

HUNTING WITH THE HANDGUN

There is a great deal of misconception in the minds of handgunners regarding the true killing power of the handgun. People who should have better judgment spin many dangerous yarns about shooting big game with the onehand gun. There isn't a pistol or revolver in existence that is fit to use on game the size of deer. A number of years ago one of our handgun manufacturers developed a new cartridge and a new revolver for the load and in order to give the development proper ballyhoo he proceeded to stalk and kill a very small moose, an equally small and unimpressive black bear and an elk. When his exploits were given the proper splash in all the outdoor magazines it served no better purpose than to encourage a good many handgunners to go afield and cripple big game.

I am an enthusiastic devotee of the hunting handgun. I enjoy nothing so much as to stalk and kill game with the pistol, however, I limit my hunting to the small things. The handgun will kill rabbits, squirrels, birds, foxes, javalina, wildcats and similar game, but it distinctly is not for such beasts as coyotes, wolves, deer, antelope and those species even larger.

An enthusiastic devotee of hunting with the handgun

I recently saw published in one of our midwestern hunting-and-fishing magazines a series of letters from three Californians who were attempting to kill deer with the .44 Special revolver. The firearms editor in publishing the series of letters was very lauditory of the purpose of the sportsmen (?). However, what was most revealing about the accounts of the two or three deer shot was that the game was running and hits had been luckily made in head or neck. How anyone could be so utterly devoid of sportsmanship as to shoot at a running buck with a handgun at distances of more than 100 yards (as these birds did) is beyond my understanding.

Experiences as a forest ranger in New Mexico   In 1929-30 I was a forest ranger in the northwest corner of New Mexico. On one side of me was the Jicarilla Apache Indian Reservation and on the other side was a goodly stretch of land in Public Domain. The Indians had a great many horses and these they permitted to run wild. Since only a part of my ranger district was fenced, these broomtails fed as much off my grass as off the Reservation. On the side which bordered the Public Domain I had little grazing problem save from nesters who wanted to slip a few head of stock onto the forest when my back was turned. The horse problem was the more serious. I estimated the Indians were running not less than 1400 head of worthless, runty, unbroken broncs on the forest land.

With the tacit approval of the forest supervisor, who was more than 100 miles away, at Taos, I declared war. Everywhere I rode, and for five months of the year I averaged 30 miles a day; I carried a sixshooter and a rifle and every time I came upon a band of broomtails I left dead horses in plentiful numbers. These animals were almost like deer. You could not ride up on them if the wind was in their favor. They would scent you and hightail it when you were a half mile away. I stalked them like a band of elk. I'd climb a hill and carefully survey the country ahead. If a band was in sight I'd get the wind in my favor approach on foot to within 50 yards, crawling the last couple of hundred yards, and then open up on them. At the first shot the band would take to its heels like antelope.

I killed several hundred horses and I used a variety of both handguns and rifles on them. I deliberately set out to prove all the larger calibers of pistols and revolvers. I used the .30 Luger, the 9 mm. Luger, the .38 Super Automatic, the .45 Auto, and even the .22 Woodsman. I also used the .38 revolver, the .38-40, .44-40, .44 Special and the .45 Colt. Unfortunately the .357 Magnum had not yet been developed. I believe it is the most powerful of all one-hand weapons and I would have enjoyed proving this contention.

As a result of my exhaustive experimenting on the Indian broomtails I hold a very low opinion of the pistol as a killer of any medium-size animal. These horses were not wild game, even though they were precious near to being so; they were born of domesticated mares. It can be safely assumed, for instance, that a runty three-year-old weighing 650 pounds could be killed more easily than a bull elk of the same poundage, or of a bear running about the same weight. Despite this, I could never kill these horses with any certainty. Many times the animal had to be finished with the rifle, which I also kept handy for that very purpose. I shot these animals everywhere, I shot them in the head, neck, shoulders, spine, through the heart, in the lungs and through the paunch. I shot them from directly in front and I shot them from behind. I had a pack of dogs that I ran lions with and so I butchered many of the jugheads for hound meat and traced the course of many of my shots.

Not only was penetration poor but the most disappointing thing was the lack of shock. This was apparent with all the calibers and with the high speed loads like the .30 Luger, 9 mm. Luger and .38 Super the lack of apparent blow was most noticeable. Of the several big calibered revolvers I liked the .38-40, .44-40 and .44 Special very much. I could see little difference in the performance of the three. It is now contended that the .44 Special can be souped up with heavy overloads so it is the best killer of them all. This is very probably true. With factory loads, which I was using, I couldn't see that it was any better than either the .38-40 or the .44-40. The .45 Colt distinctly will not kill like these other big loads.

As a result of my vast amount of experimentation on the Apaches' livestock I have a very poor opinion of the handgun as a killer of big game.

I eventually tired of living like a sheepherder

and hearing some exciting stories about the gun-
fighting that was going on along the Mexican border between the newly organized Border Patrol
and the "contrabandistas" I resigned from the Forest Service and accepted an appointment in the
Patrol. My pardner, George Parker, was already in
the outfit and was into and out of one gun fracas
after another whetting my appetite for a taste of
the excitement.

Experiences
as a mem-
ber of the
Border
Patrol

After a year in El Paso I was assigned to a
desert outpost about 25 miles west of El Paso.
The part of the International Line to be covered
by my pardner and I was ample for even the most
space-loving; we had a stretch ranging from the
outskirts of El Paso to Deming, New Mexico, 120
miles west. We ranged this area on horseback but
after a few years we put the caballos out to pas-
ture and commenced to cruise in an old sedan
equipped with giant sand tires. For a hunter
like myself it was rich existence, for every day I
was tracking game — big game — the most dangerous and therefore the most exciting of all.
We had frequent brushes with the smugglers, and
since tracking gangs in an old car was a sure invi-
tation to ambush we were kept on our toes most
of the time.

Among other dodges that we employed to track
down the border crossers, was a pack of hounds.
These kyoodles worked fairly well if we put them
on a track immediately after a rain, otherwise the
sand was so barren of moisture it would not hold

the scent for any length of time. If however, our quarry decided to strike for the Rio Grande Valley the dogs worked marvelously, for the valley was under irrigation and there the scent remained very well. Feeding the pack was a problem.

The desert was alive with jackrabbits and I killed the long-eared denizens with my sixshooter. We rode horseback about 30 miles daily, and after changing to the car drove 50-75 miles each tour. We always came in with enough jacks to feed the pups their daily big meal.

The desert jack is an animal weighing about 8-12 pounds and he is as tough as the country itself. While his body appears soft and certainly is easily penetrated with any kind of a pistol bullet, getting the game to lie down and die peacefully after you have done a thorough ventilation job is quite another thing.

During the 5 years I was stationed on the desert I killed several thousand jackrabbits. I shot them with every caliber of handgun in the book, mostly however I used the big calibers, .38 Special and larger. Unless a jack was shot through the heart or spine (I couldn't shoot well enough to hit head or neck except by sheer luck) he was dangerously apt to escape. A shot through the lungs or the paunch, or in one of the legs meant that he would run, if through the lungs not far, but if farther back he might get away entirely. One of the worst killers in this regard was the .45 ACP, a cartridge which I used in both the service automatic and in the S. & W. Model 1917 revolver. The 230 grain slug, heavily jacketed, would knock a rabbit down; he'd kick and twitch for perhaps 20 seconds and suddenly bound to his feet and be gone. I learned with this caliber that if I bowled the quarry over the thing to do was to drive in a following shot as quickly as I could.

Two of the best killers were the .44-40 and the .44 Special. When the .357 Magnum came along it killed jacks better than any of the others; the shock effect was noticeably greater. However, it left a great deal to be desired. While the gun has 1450 ft. seconds of muzzle velocity, the amount of upset to the slug when it encounters the soft flesh and flimsy bones of the western jack is insignificant. The .32-20, a low-powered rifle cartridge is infinitely better. After my many years of shooting rabbits observing as I have, the mediocre performance of even our most powerful handguns, it seems utter stupidity for anyone to consider shooting big game with sixshooter or auto pistol.

One year while returning from the National Matches I stopped off in Oklahoma and had a shoot-of-a-lifetime on bull frogs. I had with me **A shoot-of-** two members of the Border Patrol pistol team and **a-lifetime** it was the first time either had ever shot frogs with **on bull frogs** the pistol. We used our regular match .22 automatics and match ammunition. We soon learned that although shooting distances were ridiculously short a high degree of precision was required in the placement of the shot. The bullet had to hit the brain or sever the spinal cord directly behind the brain. Otherwise the greenback would give one last convulsive leap and be lost. It was exciting and interesting sport.

Probably of more fun to me was an annual pilgrimage I used to make back to Oklahoma every year to visit my father. In the woods about **Squirrel** his place were tiny fox squirrels and these I used **hunting** to stalk using a Colt Shooting Master and wadcutter loads. It was the custom — and an ironbound one, believe me — that squirrels had to be shot in the head. If someone saw you bringing in a mess of squirrels shot anywhere except in the head you were "hurrahed," to use the vernacular of the section. I therefore endeavored to drill my game through the head. The wadcutter bullet when I did connect with a sly red ear was worse than lightning. I was at that time firing away about 35,000 rounds of pistol ammunition annually and so the business of hitting a mark about 2¼ inches square at distances of 60 feet was not as difficult as it might seem.

For this shooting, the revolver I used was equipped with patridge type sights, but the front post was a red plastic made by King Gunsight Co. It loomed up in the woods beautifully; otherwise the gun was a standard target weapon.

During the years I was on the desert I lived in a tiny settlement where there were five American families and about one hundred Mexicans. About the water-pumping station (for the Southern Pacific R.R.) were a number of cottonwood trees. Here I used to shoot English sparrows. The sparrow, as everyone knows weighs about 3 ounces, maybe less, and offers a target about the size of the end of your thumb, an antimated, suspicious target never given to lingering long in any one place. I used to shoot sparrows daily and rich fun it was.

Tommy Box, a regular member of the Border Patrol pistol team, later killed in line of duty, came out one day and with my old tomcat, Pancho Villa, tagging at our heels we shot 17 sparrows. The cat ate them one by one and upon gulping down the last, I observed that the middle portions of the feline chassis were barely clearing the sand. Had someone not nearly so familiar with his nocturnal habits as myself seen him, they would most likely have immediately jumped to the conclusion that here was a pussy in the latter stages of feline pregnancy. Those 17 sparrows bulked up most startlingly and while Pancho did not die of tomcat indigestion the meal made a lasting impression on him. He never afterward could be persuaded to eat a single sparrow.

For this shooting, Box used his Woodsman .22 auto and I used a H. & R. .22 single shot furnished me by Walter Roper, who had designed the model for the Harrington and Richardson Co. The .22 was the only practical gun to use on the tiny marks.

Handguns for game shooting may be any cal-

Handguns for game can be any caliber from .22 to .45

iber from .22 to .45, the caliber depends on the wild things hunted. The .22 performs very well on such targets as small birds, crows, the lesser hawks, squirrels, cottontail rabbits, snakes, frogs, gophers, chipmunks and like small game. For targets like jack rabbits, the larger hawks, owls, fox, wildcats, javalina, mountain lions when bayed by the hounds, and game similar to this, I favor the very heaviest calibers. The gun may be revolver or automatic but should be of good weight, at least 36 ounces, and should have a barrel length running at least 5 inches. Custom stocks are a great help just as they are on target guns.

CONTRIBUTOR BIOGRAPHIES

CHARLES ASKINS, JR. — The younger Charles Askins (1907–1999) was the famous son of an even more famous father. He followed in his father's footsteps as a gun writer, authoring a number of books and serving as field editor of *Guns Magazine* for many years. He was a colorful, controversial, and often cantankerous individual who in the course of his lifetime was a solider, lawman, firearms expert, noted big game hunter, and marksmanship instructor. He won the National Pistol Championship as a young man and taught marksmanship while a member of the U.S. Border Patrol. He also saw service in World War II and trained South Vietnamese troops in Vietnam.

His books include *Hitting the Bull's-Eye* (1939), *The Art of Handgun Shooting* (1941), *Wing and Trap Shooting* (1948), *The Pistol Shooter's Book* (1953), *The Shotgunner's Book* (1958), *Texans, Guns & History* (1970), *Gunfighters* (1981), and *Unrepentant Sinner* (1985; his autobiography).

JEFF COOPER — Jeff Cooper is a marine turned writer who was an expert pistol shot. After retiring at the rank of lieutenant colonel, Cooper wrote a number of books and contributed to national magazines. His books include *Fighting Handguns* (1958), *Guns of the Old West* (1959), and *The Complete Book of Modern Handgunning* (1961). He coached a number of intraservice pistol teams and personally won numerous first places in combat pistol shooting matches. He contributed the sections on pistol shooting to Jack O'Connor's *Complete Book of Shooting* (1965).

JULIAN HATCHER — Julian Hatcher (1888–1963) grew up in Virginia's Shenandoah Valley. He graduated with honors from the U.S. Naval Academy at Annapolis, Maryland, but after a brief period in the naval service transferred to the U.S. Army. His career in that branch of the military stretched from 1910 to 1946, and throughout that time and beyond, he was recognized as one of America's leading authorities on firearms. He was an expert on everything from cannons and mortars to small arms, and he was also an inventor of some genius.

Hatcher first garnered major recognition in 1914, when he developed a highly functional breech mechanism; and in the latter stages of World War I, he oversaw military efforts connected with small arms and machine gun engineering and design. He would later be attached first to the Springfield Armory and then the Frankford Arsenal, before a stint as Army chief of ordnance, Small Arms Division, from 1929 to 1933.

It was during this period that he began to make his true mark as a writer and as an expert marksman with both pistol and rifle. Some of his earliest writing was done for the NRA's *Arms and the Man,* and he also later contributed to that magazine's successor publication, *American Rifleman.* He served as technical editor of the latter magazine for a number of years.

Over the course of his career, Hatcher wrote an impressive number of books, including *Pistols and Revolvers and Their Use* (1927), *Textbook of Pistols and Revolvers* (1935), *Handloader's Manual: A Treatise* (1937), *Hatcher's Notebook* (1947), *The Book of the Garand* (1948), *Handloading: An NRA Manual* (1950), and the posthumously published *NRA Firearms and Ammunition*

(1964). Hatcher died on December 4, 1963, and, fittingly for a man who had done stellar duty for his country in so many ways, was buried in Arlington National Cemetery.

A. L. A. HIMMELWRIGHT — Abraham Lincoln Artman Himmelwright, an architect by profession, was one of the leading authorities on pistols and pistol shooting during the first part of the twentieth century. A marksman of the first order, he captained the Americas Shooting Team at one point and also served as president of the United States Revolver Association. His literary efforts include *In the Heart of the Bitter-Root Mountains* (1895), a description of a famed Montana elk hunt by the Carlin party; the section on pistols and revolvers in Caspar Whitney (editor), *Guns, Ammunition, and Tackle* (1904); and *Pistol and Revolver Shooting* (1915). He also wrote *The San Francisco Earthquake and Fire,* which looked in depth at building materials and the lessons the disaster had to offer.

JACK O'CONNOR — Jack O'Connor (1902-1978) was born in Nogales, Arizona. After a short stint with the U.S. Army's 158th Infantry at the end of World War I, O'Connor obtained undergraduate and graduate degrees and then taught college in Texas and Arizona, all the while moonlighting by writing for newspapers and working for the Associated Press. He wrote two novels in the early 1930s, but as his family grew, O'Connor turned to writing for outdoor magazines to supplement his meager income.

It was in writing on guns and hunting that he found his métier. His love of guns and their uses in sport, along with a real feel for words and a transparent honesty that he could no more hold in check than he could hold his fiery temper, was what made O'Connor such a great writer. Most of his columns, feature articles, and books were written over the course of the three-plus decades, beginning in 1939, that he was associated with *Outdoor Life*. As the magazine's shooting editor, he was insightful, opinionated, and extremely influential. Almost single-handedly, he popularized flat-shooting, smaller-caliber rifles (most notably his beloved .270). Through his columns, he led adoring readers on hunts for all the species of North American big game, on safaris in Africa, and on shikars in Asia.

O'Connor was a complex, complicated individual. A friend, Jim Rikhoff, suggested that he was "a mixture of the sensitive and the sensible, of the ribald and reflective, of insight and inspiration, of instinct and intellect." As an author he was unquestionably a masterful stylist, and the same held true in the natty way he dressed, his feel for sportsmanship, and so many other aspects of his life.

His books are his most significant and enduring literary legacy. Here is a list of O'Connor's books, in chronological order by date of original publication: *Conquest* (1930; a novel), *Boom Town* (1931; a novel), *Game in the Desert* (1939; published with a new preface in 1945 under the title *Hunting in the Southwest*), *Hunting in the Rockies* (1947), *Sporting Guns* (1947), *The Rifle Book* (1949), *Hunting with a Binocular* (1949), *Sportsman's Arms and Ammunition Manual* (1952), *The Big-Game Rifle* (1952), *Jack O'-Connor's Gun Book* (1953), *The Outdoor Life Shooting Book* (1957), *Complete Book of Rifles and Shotguns* (1961; an excerpt was later published as *7-Lesson Rifle Shooting Course*), *The Big Game Animals of North America* (1961), *Jack O'Connor's Big Game Hunts* (1963), *Complete Book of*

Shooting (1965), *The Shotgun Book* (1965), *The Art of Hunting Big Game in North America* (1967), *Horse and Buggy West: A Boyhood on the Last Frontier* (1969), *The Hunting Rifle* (1970), *Rifle and Shotgun Shooting Basics* (1986), *Sheep and Sheep Hunting* (1974), *Game in the Desert Revisited* (limited edition, 1977; trade edition, 1984), *The Best of Jack O'Connor* (1977), *The Hunter's Shooting Guide* (1978), *Hunting Big Game* (1979), *The Last Book: Confessions of a Gun Editor* (1984), and *Hunting on Three Continents with Jack O'Connor* (1987). The latter two works were published posthumously.

In addition to being the sole author of the aforementioned works, O'Connor was a major contributor to a number of other books, most published or sponsored by *Outdoor Life*. Particularly noteworthy in this regard are his contributions to *Outdoor Life's Gallery of North American Game* (1946), *The Hunter's Encyclopedia* (1948), *The New Hunter's Encyclopedia* (1966), and *Sportsman's Encyclopedia* (1974). Selections from his writings have appeared in dozens of anthologies.

WILLIAM REICHENBACH — William Reichenbach was an exceptionally elusive figure. He does not appear in any of the standard biographical directories. Clearly he was an acquaintance of that publishing genius of the firearms world, Thomas G. Samworth, for both of Reichenbach's books, *Sixguns and Bullseyes* (1936) and *Automatic Pistol Marksmanship* (1937), were published by Samworth's Small-Arms Technical Publishing Company. He wrote in a chatty, engaging style, "blissfully ignoring all literary precepts" (according to Samworth), but his two books on pistols seem to be the extent of his work as an author.

SELECT BIBLIOGRAPHY

Army Marksmanship Unit Pistol Training Guide. Amsterdam, the Netherlands: Fredonia Books, 2001. Reprinted from 1980 edition. iv, 145 pp. Illus.

Askins, Charles [Jr.]. *The Art of Handgun Shooting.* New York: A. S. Barnes, 1941. 219 pp. Illus.

————. *The Pistol Shooter's Book: A Modern Encyclopedia.* Harrisburg, PA: Stackpole, 1953. [viii], 347 pp. Illus., index.

Chapel, Charles Edward. *The Art of Shooting.* New York: A. S. Barnes, 1960. 424 pp. Illus., index. A detailed guide to all aspects of pistol, revolver, and rifle shooting.

Cooper, Jeff. *The Complete Book of Modern Handgunning.* New York: Bramhall House, 1961. viii, 262 pp. Illus., index. Useful material from a frequent contributor to *Guns and Ammo* magazine.

Gould, Arthur C. *Modern American Pistols and Revolvers.* Plantersville, SC: Small-Arms Technical Publishing Co., 1946. 222 pp. Illus. A reprint of the 1894 edition written under the pseudonym Ralph Greenwood.

Hatcher, Julian S. *Textbook of Pistols and Revolvers.* Plantersville, SC: Small-Arms Technical Publishing Co., 1935, viii, 533 pp. Illus., index. Chapters 13 and 14 "Learning to Shoot" and "Practical Shooting," are particularly helpful.

Himmelwright, A. L. A. *Pistol and Revolver Shooting.* New York: Outing Publishing Co., 1916. No. 34 in the Outing Handbooks series. 223 pp. Illus., index. Outdated in most senses, but historically important.

Jennings, Mike. *Instinct Shooting*. New York: Dodd, Mead, 1959. 157 pp. Illus.

O'Connor, Jack. *Complete Book of Shooting.* With Roy Dunlap, Alex Kerr, and Jeff Cooper. New York: Outdoor Life, 1965. [vi], 385 pp. Illus., index. This is an important work of enduring value. Cooper's contributions on the pistol are certainly as important as O'Connor's contributions on rifles.

———. *The Hunter's Shooting Guide*. With a preface by Jim Carmichael. New York: Outdoor Life, 1978. vi, 170 pp. Illus., index. Originally published in 1957 under the title *Outdoor Life Shooting Book,* this is a collection of pieces on rifles, handguns, and shotguns. Of particular note are the chapters entitled "This Flinching Business" and "Beginning with a Handgun."

———. *Sportsman's Arms and Ammunition Manual*. Garden City, NY: Garden City Books, 1952. 256 pp. Illus., index. An overlooked O'Connor title with a three-chapter section entitled "How to Shoot Your Rifle", a six-chapter section entitled "Scopes, Sights and Sighting," and two chapters on handguns. Also published under the title *Arms and Ammunition Annual.*

Petzal, David E., ed. *The Experts' Book of the Shooting Sports*. New York: Simon & Schuster, 1972. 320 pp. Illus., index. Contributions from a number of leading authorities, with Gary Anderson's "Rifle Target Shooting" and Steve Ferber's "Handgun Target Shooting" being of particular note.

Reichenbach, William. *Automatic Pistol Marksmanship*. Plantersville, SC: Small-Arms Technical Publishing Co., 1937. viii, 140 pp. Illus. Interesting little book written in a decidedly lively style.

————. *Sixguns and Bullseyes.* Plantersville, SC: Small-Arms Technical Publishing Co., 1936. [xii], 145 pp. Illus. Quirky, written in an oddball style, and fascinating. Particularly useful on physical aspects of pistol marksmanship.

Smith, W. H. B. *The N. R. A. Book of Small Arms.* Vol. 1, *Pistols and Revolvers.* Harrisburg, PA: Military Service Publishing Co., 1946. [xxv], 638 pp. Illus., index. Comprehensive coverage devoted to various types of pistols and revolvers.

Whelan, Townsend.   *Small Arms Design and Ballistics.* Vol. 1, *Design.* Georgetown, SC: Small-Arms Technical Publishing Co., 1945, vi, 352 pp. Illus., index.

————. *Small Arms Design and Ballistics.* Vol. 2, *Ballistics.* Georgetown, SC: Small-Arms Technical Publishing Co., 1946. ix, 314 pp. Illus., index. Helpful on a variety of topics, ranging from wind deflection to care and storage of arms and ammunition.

ABOUT THE AUTHOR

Jim Casada the editor and compiler of this work, was a university history professor before taking early retirement to write full-time on hunting, fishing, and other outdoor-related topics. He serves as series editor of the Firearms Classics Library from Palladium Press and of the Outdoor Tennessee Series from the University of Tennessee Press. He is a senior editor of *Sporting Classics* magazine and a contributing editor for *The Hunting Magazine, Cabela's Outfitter Journal,* and *Sporting Clays.* He serves as editor at large for *Turkey and Turkey Hunting* and has contributed hunting and gun-related pieces to dozens of publications, including *Outdoor Life, American Hunter, North American Hunter, Sports Afield, Shooter's Bible, Deer & Deer Hunting,* and *Gun Hunter Magazine.* He has written, edited, or contributed to more than 30 books, including *The Best of Horatio Bigelow* (1994), *The Lost Classics of Robert Rourke* (1996), *Africa's Greatest Hunter* (1998), *Innovative Turkey Hunting* (2000), *Forgotten Tales and Vanished Trails* (2001); on Theodore Roosevelt as a hunter and naturalist, and a quartet of works bringing together the finest hunting writings of Archibald Rutledge. With his wife, Ann, he has coauthored a number of game cookbooks. Casada is a past president of both the Southeastern Outdoor Press Association and the Outdoor Writers Association of America.